THE SKINT COOK

OVER 80 EASY, TASTY RECIPES THAT WON'T BREAK THE BANK

THE SKINT COOK

OVER 80 EASY, TASTY RECIPES THAT WON'T BREAK THE BANK

IAN BURSNALL

SERVES 4

EASY PEASY CIDER & SAUSAGE STEW

SERVE OVER (MASHED POTATOES)

INGREDIANTS

- 8 SAUSAGES of YORE CHOICE
- 2 MEDIUM ONIONS CHOPPED
- 250 g CHOPPED INTO SMALL BITE SIZE PEACES CARROTS
- 250 g CHOPPED SWEDE INTO SMALL BITE SIZE PIECES
- 4 GARLIC CLOVES FINELY CHOPPED
- ½ TBS TOMATOE PUREE
- 1 BAY LEAF
- 1 TSP ENGLISH MUSTARD
- 1 MEDIUM APPLE SKIN ON
- ¼ TSP PEPPER
- 400 mL CHICKEN STOCK
- 250 mL DRY CIDER
- 1 TBSP PLAIN FLOUR
- 1 TSP APPLE SAUCE
- 1½ TBSP VEG OIL TO FRI VEG
- ½ TSP VEG OIL TO BROWN SAUSAGES
- SALT TO TASTE

METHOD !

IN A LARGE FRYING PAN PUT OIL IN ON MEDIUM HEAT ADD SASAGES AND BROWN ON ALL SIDES AROUND 5 MINS REMOVE AND SET ASIDE PUT REMAINING OIL IN PAN ADD ONIONS / CARROTS / SWEDE COOK UNTILL YOU START TO GET COLIOUR THEN ADD GARIC COOK A FURTHER MINUTE THEN ADD TOMATOE PUREE COOK OUT FOR 30 SECS NOW ADD FLOUR COMBINE WELL NOW ADD CIDER KEEP STIRINS TILL THERE IS NO LUMPS NOW ADD STOCK RETURN SAUSAGES AND BAY LEAF / MUSTARD / APPIE SAUCE / COOK ON MEDIUM UNTIL IT STARTS TO REDUCE STIR FROM TIME TO TIM ABOUT 5 TO 7 MINS BEFORE READY ADD APPIE AND PEPPER DONT WANT THE APPIE TO MUSH DOWN I LIKE THE APPIE TO STIL HAVE A BITE CHECK FOR SALT YOU MIGHT NOT NEED ANY ITS DONE WHEN THE VEG IS JUST TENDER AND SAUCE HAS THICKENED (YOU MAY HAVE TO TOP UP WITH WATER) REMOVE BAY LEAF

CONTENTS

INTRODUCTION

Growing up there were seven of us: my mum and dad, Dale, Jonny, Mark, Emma and me. We were a typical old-school family. My dad went out grafting 60 hours a week (sometimes 70) to support us and my mum looked after us, cooking and cleaning, getting us ready for school, etc.

I think my love of cooking comes from my mum. She's a great cook. We grew up on big hearty stews, roast dinners, home-made soups, toad-in-the-hole... all your typical classics. Being a big family, money was tight, but my mum had the ability to stretch ingredients a long way, using all sorts of tricks. We never went hungry, that's for sure.

When I turned eighteen and moved out, my mum gave me a load of pots and pans and handwritten recipes. I still have them to this day. I think the first thing I cooked was chilli con carne. If I ever got stuck or needed advice, I could always ring her up on the house phone (there were no mobile phones then, and not much internet either).

Every weekend my mates would come round and I would cook. They seemed to love it. I don't know if it's because we were all steaming or not, but it gave me a buzz and I really got hooked. Those were great times with the lads. I wouldn't change them for all the money in the world!

After living on my own for a couple of years, a new neighbour moved in. I used to play music a bit too loud. One day I was on my way out to the pub and the neighbour stopped me getting into a taxi and said, 'Can you stop playing loud music?' (Well, something along those lines. I can't print what was actually said...!) I said I was sorry and went to the pub. The taxi driver, having heard what was said, told me to go back later and apologise properly. So I did... and the neighbour is now my partner, Donna! Twenty-seven years on and we're still together - all because of loud music and a taxi driver.

Soon we moved in together and along came our princess, Liv (Olivia Rose). Then four years later our adorable son, Toby. We were old school as well. I went out grafting for us and Donna looked after Liv and Toby. Money was, and still is, tight, but we ate well on a budget. It must have been my mum's and dad's methods and ways that rubbed off on us - great cooking and hard work.

In the last several years I've been struggling with health issues, which has affected my roofing job. My stepsister Karen said to me, 'Why don't you start an Instagram page showing off your food?' I came up with the name 'The Skint Roofer Cook' (I was skint and a roofer), which caught the attention of a production company. They asked me to apply for a cooking show about winning a book deal, so I sent in a video with my ideas.

I thought the video was awful. I'd just lost my close friend Ken, and was suffering from a hangover, so I didn't think it would lead to anything. But they must have liked what they saw, because they contacted me to say I'd made it through to the next stage. At this point they mentioned that Jamie Oliver was involved. That's when I thought, 'This is a game changer' - which had been my friend Ken's favourite saying! It was almost like he was looking down on me.

Anyway, I got on the show: *The Great Cookbook Challenge* with Jamie Oliver. I was bricking it. I wanted to get past the first round so badly but didn't think I was good enough. Still, I thought, 'Just be yourself and go for it' - which I did, and much to my surprise I got through. After that, I went into each round with the same principle: be yourself, and what you see is what you get. (I wear my heart on my sleeve!)

I managed to get to the final. At this point, I was just happy it was bringing me exposure, which is priceless. I cooked Donna's favourite dish: Stilton roast spuds. They went down a storm with the nation, featuring in newspapers and magazines. I didn't win - I was a runner-up with Rex, and Dominique won (and a worthy winner as well). Thank you to all involved in the show. The big man himself, Jamie Oliver, is one top, top geezer. He's got a heart of gold and was a true inspiration during the final.

After the show finished, I was inundated with book offers - I was getting hundreds of messages a day. I couldn't keep up with them all. But the one that stood out to me was from Lisa Milton, executive publisher at HQM&B. We arranged to chat, and I was so impressed. She is the real deal. She told me how her whole family had wanted me to win, but she hadn't - because she wanted to publish me! What a story. Lisa introduced me to the team at Bev James Management, who now represent me. I couldn't have better people looking out for me. Lisa offered me a book deal and together we all made it happen. Thank you for believing in me, Lisa and the team at Bev James.

My book is based on easy but banging flavours, with recipes inspired by my life. I want people to fall in love with cooking. Cook one of my recipes and get a pat on the back - it will give you a buzz and make you want to cook again. Remember, do the simple things right and you're halfway there.

Never stop chasing your dreams, no matter your age - the dreams aren't going to chase you!

I hope you enjoy cooking from my book half as much as I enjoyed making it.

Much love to you all,

HOW I COOK AND LIKE TO EAT

- I try not to pre-plan meals too far in advance. Some days I wake up and think I am going to cook a toad-in-the-hole, but when I get to the supermarket there's all sorts on offer, so I end up doing peri peri chicken on the barbecue instead. It's good to cook on impulse because it releases your creative side. If you plan out your meals for every day of the week and stick with them, it becomes so boring, so cook what you fancy and use what you see on offer to inspire you. Also ask what your family might like - it's always nice to know what they are in the mood for as well.

- When we decide to have something like a roast, with multiple elements, Donna will prep all the veg and will make the sausage meat stuffing, while I am in charge of the meat and things like leek sauce, braised red cabbage, cauliflower cheese, etc. It is worth splitting the tasks and playing to your strengths - doing the things that you enjoy.

- Also, don't be embarrassed if you have freezer food a few times a week or use frozen Yorkshires or powdered gravy. They are brilliant shortcuts, and used from time to time they can make your life easier. Remember, cooking should be enjoyable, you don't have to cook from scratch all the time; you need a night off every now and then.

STORECUPBOARD ESSENTIALS

This is a list of storecupboard essentials that I use on a weekly basis and recommend purchasing if you're just starting your journey into cooking (hopefully, you may already have some of these on your shelves!). Remember, if you're buying them all at once (it's quite a long list, so do not feel you have to!), it's short-term pain but long-term gain. They will last forever in the cupboard, so it's money well spent.

Alternatively, you can of course build up your storecupboard by buying a few of these ingredients every week for a few months and spread the cost (and save some space). Also, when friends and family ask you what you want for birthdays and Christmas, why not ask for some storecupboard ingredients? They would be great (and useful) presents.

And don't forget to look out for supermarket own-brand foods. For stuff like pasta, rice, canned veg, herbs, spices and sauces, buying own brand can make a big difference.

THE BASICS

- [ ] Table salt and flaky salt
- [ ] Black pepper
- [ ] Garlic powder
- [ ] Onion powder
- [ ] Olive oil
- [ ] Vegetable oil

HERBS

- [ ] Dried thyme
- [ ] Dried oregano
- [ ] Dried rosemary
- [ ] Dried basil
- [ ] Dried sage
- [ ] Bay leaves

SPICES

- [ ] Chilli powder
- [ ] Chilli flakes
- [ ] Paprika
- [ ] Smoked paprika
- [ ] Curry powder
- [ ] Ground cumin
- [ ] Ground coriander
- [ ] Ground turmeric
- [ ] Chinese five spice powder
- [ ] Fennel seeds
- [ ] Ground ginger
- [ ] Ground cinnamon
- [ ] Ground nutmeg
- [ ] Ground allspice

DRY GOODS

- ☐ Pasta (e.g. macaroni, lasagne sheets)
- ☐ Rice (e.g. basmati, jasmine)
- ☐ Noodles (e.g. dried egg noodles)
- ☐ Plain flour
- ☐ Self-raising flour
- ☐ Cornflour
- ☐ Caster sugar
- ☐ Soft brown sugar (light and dark)

CANNED GOODS

- ☐ Canned tomatoes
- ☐ Canned sweetcorn
- ☐ Canned kidney beans
- ☐ Canned butter beans
- ☐ Canned peas
- ☐ Canned carrots
- ☐ Baked beans

CONDIMENTS

- ☐ Soy sauce
- ☐ Malt vinegar
- ☐ Balsamic vinegar
- ☐ Cider vinegar
- ☐ Shaoxing rice wine
- ☐ Worcestershire sauce
- ☐ Wholegrain mustard
- ☐ American mustard
- ☐ Dijon mustard
- ☐ Tomato ketchup
- ☐ Tomato purée
- ☐ Sesame oil

KITCHEN EQUIPMENT

There is some kitchen equipment it's hard to live without. This is a list of what I consider essential. You never know, you probably already have quite a few of them tucked away somewhere. These are the items that will prove helpful if you have them to hand or can borrow from a friend or neighbour, but I don't expect you to go out and buy them all!

ESSENTIALS

☐ A meat thermometer

Hands down, this is a must. I cannot recommend having one of these enough - it could be make or break, especially for roast meats. Yes, you can follow timings from a recipe, but not every oven is the same - it could be hotter or colder than the temperature it is set on. The meat could be underdone, which is a no-no with chicken, or it could be overdone (especially if you prefer cooking beef to your liking). Let's face it, you are paying good money for meat, so you want it to be just right. With a meat thermometer, you will reliably be able to cook the meat to the desired temperature every time.

MY OTHER MUST-HAVES

- A good set of (sharp!) knives
- 3 chopping boards - one each for meat, fish, salad/veg
- Kitchen scales
- Measuring spoons
- Good set of pots and pans with lids
- Non-stick frying pan
- Large pan or wok
- Griddle pan
- 2-3 roasting tins (one big, one medium and/or small)
- Baking sheets
- Wire rack (for cooling)
- Yorkshire pudding tin (or muffin tin)
- Cake, muffin and tart tins (various sizes)

- 1 large and 2-3 small ovenproof dishes
- Ovenproof ramekins
- Big and small mixing bowls
- Measuring jug
- Colander
- Sieve
- Grater
- Pestle and mortar
- Rolling pin
- 2 heatproof spatulas (big and small)
- Wooden spoon
- Slotted spoon
- Fish slice
- Whisk

- Potato masher
- Vegetable peeler
- Zester
- Pastry brush
- Egg cups
- Cocktail sticks (great for checking cakes)
- Can opener
- Bottle opener (a must!)
- Metal biscuit cutters
- Serving dishes
- Large serving dish or tray for Christmas turkey (I love Christmas)
- Big serving spoon
- Serving fork
- Serving tongs
- Pizza cutter (great to use on pastry)
- Blender (or food processor)
- Slow cooker
- Foil
- Clingfilm
- Greaseproof paper
- Baking paper
- Plastic storage bowls/containers with lids (we save plastic take-away ones with lids)

NON-ESSENTIALS

There are no such things as non-essentials. If something is going to transfer your dish from Sunday League to Champions League, even if it's only once or twice a year, then you need it. Everything has a purpose.

TIPS AND TRICKS

TIPS FOR COOKING ON A BUDGET

This book is packed with the good sense, good value recipes that our mums and dads and grans and grandads were raised on. It's all about getting back to basics, using what you have and creating big, hearty, wholesome meals with ingredients that are accessible at prices that are affordable. There's updates on classics, flavour combinations to die for and new recipes that are about to become your go-to staples. And it does this with a showcase of tricks and twists that are both ingeniously simple and incredibly effective. Whether it's swapping butter for margarine, using up a glut of apples from your neighbour's apple tree or turning leftover doughnuts into the bread pudding of your dreams, this book shows you how to get resourceful and make cooking on a budget a sustainable part of your everyday lifestyle. Here are a few tips that will hopefully make all of these recipes even more budget-friendly.

- When shopping, always look out for the reduced yellow stickers. We all love a bargain, right?!

- Eggs. Remember, the fresher the egg, the more dense the albumen (egg white) will be, which means better results when poaching and frying. Older eggs are the best for boiling, as they are easier to peel.

- Avoid buying too much reduced-price food, especially if you have no room left in the freezer. I know it's tempting but it will probably go out of date before you use it. It's a good idea to have a look at what you already have in the freezer and start planning ways to use it, and in doing so make space for more.

- After making a salad, always wrap leftover cut veg (lettuce, cucumber, tomatoes, onion, etc.) in clingfilm before putting them back in the fridge. This will keep them fresher for longer.

- Always check your cupboards, shelves and fridge and keep them all tidy. Make a list of what you already have if you tend to buy things on impulse. You will probably find you already have three of some things - I am guilty of doing that.

- Me and my mate Nige ring each other up when we're out food shopping to tell each other when/ where there's a bargain and ask if either wants any of them. Think about who else might like some, and remember, a bargain shared is double the win!

- Start up a local friendly supper club and take it in turns to entertain or get together. It not only spreads the cost but, most importantly, connects you with the people you love, like friends and family.

LOOK OUT FOR THESE!

WHAT TO FREEZE TO USE LATER

SAUSAGES

Great to have ready for barbecues or toad-in-the-hole.

CARROTS, PARSNIPS, BRUSSELS SPROUTS, ETC.

In fact, most root veg, as you can blanch them in boiling water for a few minutes, then refresh in cold water, bag them up into portions, freeze and use when needed. At Christmas, me and our friends, Nige and Carol, go halves on a few big veg sacks from the Christmas market and do this. I love Christmas. Happy days.

CANNED VEGETABLES

For canned vegetables that are nearly out of date, take them out of the can, blanch and refresh them, then portion up and freeze.

ORANGES AND LEMONS

Cut into wedges and freeze to make instant flavoured ice cubes for your cocktails and drinks.

PORK CHOPS AND CHICKEN THIGHS

These are ideal to have on hand as a helpful standby for barbecues, grills, casseroles, etc.

CHEESE (THAT WILL FREEZE) AND MILK

Freeze suitable hard cheese in blocks or pre-grated.

BREAD

Fresh and stale - handy to have slices to make a quick late-night toastie snack; make stale bread into breadcrumbs or dice (for croutons) before freezing.

TIPS FOR COOKING WITH/FOR KIDS

- It's a great idea to get the kids involved from an early age. It's fun but also gives them an understanding of how and where food comes from, i.e. not just out of the freezer or packet and onto the plate. Get them to try the food when prepping a recipe – things like carrots, peppers, salad, etc. It will give them some understanding of how it tastes before it's cooked, and to try different tastes and textures. I hope it goes without saying, but don't let them try raw meat!

- If you have picky eaters, you can hide a lot of veg by grating it into dishes like shepherd's pie, cottage pie and spaghetti dishes or pasta sauces. This way the veg sort of disappears into the dish so they can't pick it out but are still getting the benefits from the veg.

- Blended home-made soups are also a great way to add veg and meat without the kids really knowing. Or if they have a favourite canned soup, put it into a blender with cooked veg and a little water and blend before heating it up – they'll never know!

- Why not juice (or purée) fruit (fresh or canned) and make fruit juice ice lollies? They're fun to make and tasty as well.

- Blend peeled bananas and make into banana ice lollies, then turn out of the moulds and dip one end of each into melted chocolate (it will quickly set). This will make them more appealing, as all kids like chocolate.

TIPS FOR DINNER PARTIES/GET-TOGETHERS

- Make simple recipes, ones you can make in advance like lasagne, chilli con carne and fish pie, and desserts like crumbles, cheesecakes, banoffee pie, baked sweet tarts. These can all be made in the morning or even the day before. Just pop them into the fridge until you need to cook them, or serve desserts like the banoffee pie and cheesecake (no-bake desserts) as they are.

- Simple starters like home-made soups and prawn cocktails are ace ideas, plus they're stress-free.

- Don't try out new recipes for the first time or make recipes you are not comfortable with. Cook something that you have made before and are confident about (leave the experimentation or trying out new recipes for another time). Your guests are not expecting Michelin-starred food and if they are, you're mixing with the wrong friends. I've tried to outdo myself before, and believe you me, it was carnage and not very enjoyable. Again, simple things done right is the answer.

- Another idea is to ask friends to bring starters and puddings. That way, you can focus on the main dish and give it all your effort.

- Know your limits as to how many people you invite. One year I cooked Christmas dinner for 18. Yes, 18. Don't ask me what I was thinking - anyone would have thought I had a restaurant, not a humble house kitchen. We all got fed, although it might not all have been very warm.

BARBECUE PARTY

- ☐ If you're doing a barbecue, plan to cook more than you need as you can feast on the tasty leftovers during the week. You could make great sandwiches for work (it beats a floppy cheese sandwich hands down). Also ask people to bring something along - it not only cuts the cost, but they can also take home some leftovers, plus people like to help and chip in, so it's a winner all round.

PIZZA NIGHT

- ☐ If you're having a pizza night, prep all your toppings in advance, then when you are ready to cook, encourage your friends to make their own pizzas. You might be surprised at what concoctions are made and, yes, I love pineapple on a pizza! This is a great idea if your kids have friends around as well. Fun times!

MENU
SUGGESTIONS

VEGGIE FEAST

STARTER

Curried Corn & Fried Eggs on Toast
(see page 45)

MAIN

Easy Coconut Cauliflower Curry
(see page 72)

SIDE

Bombay Roast Potatoes
(see page 144)

PUDDING

The Afterburn - Chilli Chocolate Bark
(see page 212)

FRIDAY NIGHT TREAT MENU

STARTER

Prawn Cocktail with Crispy Bacon
(see page 90)

MAIN

Steaks with Home-made Peppercorn
and Brandy Sauce (see page 67)
with Balsamic Cherry Tomatoes (see page 138)
and Garlic and Herb Crushed Potatoes (see page 145)

SIDE

The Vampire Slayer (garlic bread) (see page 157)

PUDDING

Blackberry Fool and Ginger Nut Topping
(see page 195)

ENJOY!

SUNDAY DINNER MENU

STARTER

Potato and Leek Soup with Garlic Croutons
(see page 92)

MAIN

Garlic and Herb Roast Butter Chicken
with Pan Gravy (see page 104)

SIDES

Don's Fave Stilton Spuds (see page 146)
Cauliflower Cheese (see page 158)
Sausage Meat and Cider Stuffing (see page 161)
Orange Honey Butter Carrots (see page 141)

PUDDING

The Pear of the Cob - Pear Cobbler (see page 200)

ENJOY!

WEEKEND TREAT

GRANNY D'S WEEKENDER EGG CUSTARD TART (SEE PAGE 214)

This is a must and great for every weekend. When growing up, my Granny D made it every weekend for us all. Have a slice with a cup of tea when you've finished your chores or been for a walk. Big up Granny D! x

- DIPPY EGGS WITH STILTON SOLDIERS (CREAMED WONION ON SIDE?
- TURKISH EGGS WITH A TWIST BLACK PUDDING BACON
- CURRIED CORN & FRIED EGG ON TOAST ✓
- SOME SORT OF OMELETE
- ~~GARLIC MUSHROOMS & SPINACH ON TOAST~~ ✓
  ~~WITH SUT BOILED EGG~~ (COULD USE FROZEN) SPINACH
- COTTAGE CHEESE ON TOAST WITH ROASTED
  TOMATOS & GARLIC (SWEET CHILLI DRESSN)
- (BLT? CLASSIC)   BAGELS
- LEMONY OLIVIE & CREAM CHEESE ON ~~TOAST~~
- CHEESY SAUSAGE TOAST
- CORN BEEF HASH WITH POCHED EGGS
- PIMPED UP BEANS ON TOAST POTATOE ROSTI?
- OVERNISHT OATS (TO BE DECIDED)

- BREVILE TOASTIE IDEARS THE HAWIAN
- BUBLE AND SQUEK WITH POCHED EGG ✓
- BLACK PUDDINS AND BLACKBERRY COMPOTE
  WITH PANCAKES
- FUFFY PANCAKES WITH CRISPY FRIED EGGS
  AND MANGO SALSA. ✓
  ~~CREAM CHEESE AND GARI MUSHROOM ON TO~~
  MUSHROOM & GARLIC ~~OR~~ SPINACH ON TOAST ✓
  USE CREAM CHESE FOR A SAUCE

  SMOKED HADDOCK OPEN OMELTTE AND LEMON

BREAKFAST

DIPPY EGGS WITH STILTON SOLDIERS

SERVES 2

Who doesn't like a dippy egg and soldiers? The Stilton takes it to the next level.

4 slices of bread (of your choice)

butter, for the toast (optional)

about 220g Stilton cheese, sliced or crumbled

4 medium eggs

salt and pepper

Preheat the grill to high.

Toast the bread, then place on a baking tray. Butter the toast, if you like. Cover the toast with Stilton (use as much or as little as you want), then place under the hot grill and grill until bubbling and golden. Put to one side to cool a little and firm up.

Meanwhile, put your eggs into a saucepan and cover with cold water. Place over a high heat. As soon as the eggs have come to the boil, reduce the heat to medium and set a timer for 3 minutes.

In the meantime, cut your Stilton toast into soldiers and put onto plates. When 3 minutes is up, drain the eggs and run cold water over them for 10 seconds. Now put the eggs into egg cups. Take off the top of the eggs and season to taste with salt and pepper. Start dipping!

 You may not use all the cheese, but if not, you can use it for something else or you can freeze it. Everyone is different as to how much cheese they want.

BUBBLE & SQUEAK TOPPED WITH POACHED EGGS

SERVES 2-3

What a combo and a great way to use up leftover veg. Crispy bubble and squeak topped off with a poached egg. Delightful.

400g potatoes, peeled and cut into bite-sized chunks

1 tsp salt

200g white cabbage

200g Brussels sprouts

pinch of ground nutmeg

1 tbsp vegetable oil, plus extra if needed

½ tbsp unsalted butter

2-3 eggs

salt and pepper

Rinse the potato chunks under cold running water. Place in a saucepan, cover with water, add the measured salt and bring to the boil. Cook until the potatoes are just tender, about 15-20 minutes. Drain and let them steam dry. Put to one side.

Meanwhile, chop up the cabbage and cut the Brussels in half, then put both into a saucepan. Cover with water and bring to the boil, then cook until just tender with still a bit of a bite, about 8-10 minutes. Drain. Save the water, if you like – you could use it in a stock. Let the veg steam dry.

Mix the potatoes with the cabbage and Brussels. Try to keep it chunky. Season to taste with salt, pepper and the nutmeg.

Melt the oil and butter in a frying pan over a medium heat. Put the bubble and squeak mixture in. Don't be tempted to keep moving it around as you want to build up crispy bits. Once the bottom starts to colour, you can now stir. Repeat several times until the mixture is really crispy. You may need to add a little more oil along the way. Check again for seasoning.

Meanwhile, poach the eggs following the method on page 57. Spoon the bubble and squeak into the middle of the serving plates. Serve with a poached egg on top seasoned with salt and pepper.

FLUFFY PANCAKES WITH CRISPY FRIED EGGS & MANGO SALSA

SERVES 4

This recipe takes a little more time and effort but boy does it deliver in flavours! Definitely worth the effort.

200g self-raising flour

1½ tsp baking powder

1 tbsp caster sugar

7 eggs (3 for batter, 4 to fry)

200ml milk

30g butter, melted, plus extra knobs for frying pancakes

½ tsp vanilla extract

3 tbsp vegetable oil, plus extra for frying pancakes

salt and pepper

Mango Salsa (see page 160), to serve

½ tbsp chopped parsley, to garnish

Put the flour, baking powder, sugar, 3 of the eggs, the milk, melted butter, vanilla extract, a good pinch of salt and a good grind of pepper into a bowl and mix well to a smooth batter. Let it stand for 1 hour. Put in the fridge if you let it stand for longer.

To cook the pancakes, melt a knob of butter and ½ teaspoon of the extra vegetable oil in a frying pan over a low-medium heat. Spoon 2-3 dollops of the batter into the pan, depending on the size of your pan. Cook on one side until you start to see bubbles forming on top. Check underneath - it should be golden. Flip and cook for another minute or two on the other side. Transfer to a warm plate. Repeat until all the batter has been used - you will probably need to add more butter and oil a few times. When all the pancakes are cooked, transfer to a low oven to keep warm.

Heat the 3 tablespoons of oil in a frying pan over a medium-high heat. When the oil starts to smoke, crack in the remaining 4 eggs. Be careful as the oil will spit. Start to baste your eggs with the oil and cook them to your liking (I like mine crispy on the bottom).

To serve, take 3 pancakes for each portion and place on serving plates, overlapping or in a stack. Place a fried egg on top, then spoon some mango salsa around the pancakes. Garnish with the parsley.

GARLICKY SPINACH & MUSHROOMS ON TOAST

SERVES 2

Frozen spinach is a must to have at hand. Just pop it out of the freezer any time of year. Fuss and stress-free.

80g frozen spinach

1 tbsp vegetable oil

180g closed cup mushrooms, sliced

4 garlic cloves, finely chopped

100g cream cheese

½ tsp Worcestershire sauce

good pinch of ground nutmeg

2 slices of crusty bread

butter or olive oil, for the toast (optional)

salt and pepper

Put the spinach into a saucepan, cover with water and bring to the boil. Stir until the spinach has come apart, then take off the heat, drain and put to one side.

Now put the vegetable oil into a frying pan over a medium-high heat. When the oil is smoking, add the mushrooms and stir. Press the mushrooms down for 30 seconds, then stir. Repeat two or three times until they have a great colour to them.

Add the garlic and cook for 1 minute, then add 50ml of water and cook for 1 minute. Add the cream cheese, stirring until melted. Now squeeze out the excess water from the spinach, put it in the pan and stir. Add the Worcestershire sauce, nutmeg and a good pinch each of salt and pepper. Keep stirring until the mix is reduced to the consistency of your liking.

Toast your bread, place on plates and spread it with butter or drizzle with olive oil, if you like. Spread the mushroom mixture all over and serve.

LEMONY OLIVES & CREAM CHEESE ON BAGELS

SERVES 2

This one's great for breakfast on a hot summer's morning sitting outside in the sun just chilling. It's also a nice brunch idea.

2 bagels

zest of ½ small lemon

1 tbsp lemon juice

1 tbsp olive oil

½ tsp honey

1 x 200g pack cream cheese

25g pitted black olives, sliced

salt and pepper

Cut the bagels in half and toast. Mix together the lemon zest, lemon juice, olive oil, honey and a pinch each of salt and pepper, mixing it hard so it emulsifies.

Now spread as much or as little of the cream cheese onto the toasted bottom bagel halves. Scatter over the olives and drizzle the dressing all over. Place the bagel lids on and enjoy.

CURRIED CORN & FRIED EGGS ON TOAST

SERVES 2

This is such an easy and cheap recipe, but it definitely delivers on flavour. I developed this for *The Great Cookbook Challenge.*

1 x 200g can sweetcorn

1 tbsp vegetable oil

2 slices of bread (of your choice)

½ red onion, chopped

2 garlic cloves, crushed

½ red chilli, finely chopped

½ green chilli, finely chopped

1 tbsp medium curry powder

2 tbsp unsalted butter

2 eggs

salt and pepper

1 tbsp chopped coriander, to garnish

Drain the sweetcorn and tip into a saucepan. Add ½ tablespoon of the oil and cook over a medium heat to warm through.

Meanwhile, toast your bread.

Now add the onion, garlic and chillies to the sweetcorn. Fry for a few minutes, then stir in the curry powder. Cook for a minute, then add the butter and cook for a few more minutes. You can add 1 tablespoon of water, if you like, depending on how loose you want it to be. Season to taste with salt and pepper. Put to one side and keep warm.

Put the remaining ½ tablespoon of oil into a frying pan and fry the eggs to your liking.

Put the toast onto plates, place the fried eggs on top and spoon the sweetcorn mixture all over. Garnish with the chopped coriander. Tuck in.

SMOKED HADDOCK OPEN OMELETTE WITH LEMON MUSTARD MAYONNAISE

SERVES 2

The zing of the lemon mustard mayo goes so well with this tasty smoked haddock omelette.

200g frozen smoked haddock fillet

1 tbsp vegetable oil

6 eggs

100g cherry tomatoes, quartered

½ red onion, sliced

100g Cheddar cheese, grated

3 tbsp mayonnaise

½ tsp English mustard

juice of ½ lemon

2 handfuls of watercress

salt and pepper

Cook the haddock according to the pack instructions, then put to one side.

Preheat the grill to high.

Put half the oil into a frying pan over a medium heat. Crack 3 eggs into a bowl and whisk. Pour into the pan and cook, pulling the eggs from the side of the pan into the middle, repeating until there is no liquid egg left. Remove from the heat.

Flake half the smoked haddock over the omelette. Now sprinkle half the tomatoes and half the onion over the top. Season with salt and pepper and sprinkle half the cheese over. Place under the hot grill until the cheese is nice and bubbling. Transfer to a plate and keep warm while you cook the second omelette in the same way.

Meanwhile, mix the mayonnaise, mustard, lemon juice and 1 teaspoon of water together in a small bowl and season with a good pinch each of salt and pepper.

To serve, put a handful of watercress over each omelette and drizzle the lemon mustard mayonnaise all over.

CORNED BEEF HASH WITH CHIMICHURRI, TOPPED WITH A CRISPY FRIED EGG

SERVES 4

The chimichurri takes this classic to another level. You need to crisp up the corned beef first. So many people put it in towards the end – all you get then is a pile of mush! This is a great one for brunch.

about 5 tbsp vegetable oil

1 x 340g can corned beef, cut into bite-sized chunks

700g potatoes, skin on, cut into small chunks

½ red pepper, deseeded and cut into chunks

½ yellow pepper, deseeded and cut into chunks

½ onion, chopped

3 garlic cloves, chopped

1½ tbsp smoked paprika

1 tsp ground cumin

½ tsp salt

½ tsp pepper

1 tbsp Worcestershire sauce

4 eggs

For the chimichurri

1 x 30g pack parsley, chopped

2 tbsp chopped red onion

2 garlic cloves, chopped

½ tbsp dried oregano

juice of ½ lemon

½ tsp chilli flakes

5 tbsp olive oil

2 tbsp white wine vinegar

2 tbsp honey

¼ tsp salt

¼ tsp pepper

Start by mixing all the chimichurri ingredients together in a bowl, then put to one side.

Now, for the corned beef hash, put 1 tablespoon of the vegetable oil in a frying pan over a medium-high heat. Add the corned beef to the pan and fry. It will start to go soft, so then flatten it with a spatula. When it starts to colour, stir and leave until it starts to colour again. Keep doing this until the corned beef is really crispy - I mean really crispy. This will take about 5-8 minutes. Remove from the pan to a plate and put to one side to cool.

Meanwhile, rinse the potatoes, then put into a saucepan, cover with water and bring to the boil. Boil for 5 minutes, then drain and let them steam dry for 5 minutes.

In the same pan you cooked the corned beef, heat 2 tablespoons of the vegetable oil over a medium-high heat. Add the potatoes, stir to coat in the oil and leave to cook. When they start to colour, stir. Keep repeating until they are all nicely coloured, about 5-8 minutes.

Now add the peppers and onion and stir, then cook for around 3 minutes. If you think you need to add more oil, add some. Next, stir in the garlic, paprika, cumin, salt and pepper. Now add back the corned beef, then add the Worcestershire sauce and stir. Turn off the heat and keep warm while you cook your eggs.

Put the remaining 2 tablespoons of vegetable oil into a separate frying pan over a medium-high heat. When it is smoking, crack your eggs into the pan and cook to your liking - keep basting the eggs. They are done when the bottom is nice and crispy, but they've still got a runny yolk.

To serve, spoon the corned beef hash onto plates or into bowls. Top each portion with a crispy fried egg and spoon over some chimichurri.

 Put your can of corned beef into the fridge the day before. It's easier to cut up that way.

THE ULTIMATE BRUNCH BAGEL

SERVES 2

The more you follow this technique with the scrambled eggs, the more you will get a feel for how you like your eggs. They are so deliciously silky smooth.

2 sausages (of your choice), skin removed

½ tbsp vegetable oil

120g black pudding, skin removed

½ tbsp unsalted butter

4 eggs, beaten

1 bagel, cut in half

salt and pepper

1 tbsp chopped parsley, to garnish

For the sweet chilli and garlic sauce

5 tbsp white wine vinegar

1½ tbsp caster sugar

2 garlic cloves, finely chopped

¼ tsp chilli flakes

good pinch of salt

good pinch of pepper

Put all the sauce ingredients into a small saucepan with 4 tablespoons of water and set over a medium-low heat. Bring to a simmer and stir. Let it reduce until it coats the back of a spoon, then remove from the heat and put to one side. You may have to reheat the sauce to loosen it before serving.

Meanwhile, put your sausage meat into a frying pan with the vegetable oil. Cook over a medium heat for around 3-4 minutes, breaking the meat up with a spatula. Now crumble in the black pudding, then stir and cook until the sausage meat and black pudding are cooked, around 8-10 minutes in total. Transfer to a plate and keep warm in a low oven.

Now put the butter into a cold saucepan, then put over a low heat. When the butter is melted, pour in your eggs and keep stirring. Keep taking the pan on and off the heat while stirring all the time. When you have nice and silky eggs, season with salt and pepper. It's a good idea to take the pan off the heat just before you think they're done as the eggs will carry on cooking.

While the eggs are scrambling, toast the bagel halves. Put a toasted bagel half on each plate. Spoon over the scrambled eggs, then spoon over the sausage and black pudding mix. Drizzle with the sauce (reheated first, if necessary) and sprinkle over the parsley to garnish.

THE MESSY ONE - BLT

SERVES 2

Does exactly what is says on the tin. Maximum flavour but be prepared to get messy.

4 tbsp mayonnaise

2 tbsp drained, chopped gherkins

½ tbsp gherkin juice

½ tbsp sriracha sauce

6 rashers smoked streaky bacon

1 large tomato, sliced into 6

splash of balsamic vinegar

2 croissants

60g iceberg lettuce, shredded

¼ red onion, sliced

salt and pepper

Preheat the grill to high.

Mix together the mayonnaise, gherkins, gherkin juice, sriracha and a pinch each of salt and pepper in a bowl. Put to one side.

Now arrange the bacon rashers on a baking tray and place under the hot grill. After around 5 minutes, flip the bacon, then rub the tomato slices in the bacon fat. Place the tomatoes on the tray alongside the bacon. Season with salt and pepper. Splash the tomatoes with balsamic vinegar and place back under the grill. When the bacon is nice and crispy and the tomatoes have a bit of char, remove and put to one side.

Cut your croissants in half. Dip the cut sides in the bacon fat and put under the grill to toast up.

To assemble, spread some mayo sauce on the bottom halves of the croissants. Put some lettuce and onion on top, then the bacon, followed by the tomatoes. Spoon more mayo sauce all over and put the croissant lids on. Enjoy. Definitely messy.

BIG IS BEAUTIFUL SCOTCH EGGS

SERVES 2

The trick to this awesome dish is to master the eggs so that you get that runny gooey yolk. It's a showstopper.

3 sausages (of your choice)

60g black pudding, skin removed

15g dried sage and onion stuffing mix

¼ tsp salt

¼ tsp pepper

2 whole eggs, plus 1 egg, beaten

30g plain flour

1 slice of bread, processed into breadcrumbs

vegetable oil, for frying

2 handfuls of rocket leaves, to serve

For the dressing

4 tbsp mayonnaise

1 tbsp brown sauce

1 tsp malt vinegar

½ tsp Worcestershire sauce

pinch of salt

pinch of pepper

Take the skin off the sausages and place the meat in a bowl. Crumble the black pudding in and add the stuffing mix, salt and pepper. Mix well, then put in the fridge to chill.

Meanwhile, place the 2 whole eggs in a saucepan. Cover with water, then bring to the boil. As soon as it's boiling, turn down to a slow boil and set a timer for 3 minutes. As soon as the timer is done, drain away the water and run a cold tap over the eggs for 5 minutes. Gently crack the eggs on the side of the pan and carefully peel.

Now take half of the sausage mixture and flatten into a rough circle. Place one egg in the middle and fold the sausage mixture around the egg to enclose it. Be gentle. Roll the coated egg in the flour, then the beaten egg, then the breadcrumbs to coat all over. Repeat to make the second Scotch egg.

Heat at least 3 inches of vegetable oil in a medium-sized frying pan over a medium to high heat until hot. Add the Scotch eggs to the pan and cook for around 8 minutes, turning occasionally. When they're nice and golden all over and cooked through, take out and drain on kitchen paper. Put to one side.

Now mix all the dressing ingredients together. Cut the Scotch eggs in half; you should have a nice runny yolk. Place on plates with a handful of rocket leaves and spoon the dressing over.

HASH BROWNS & DIPPING SAUCE

SERVES 2-4

These are great to share. The dipping sauce is kinda like the Big Mac sauce but better.

750g potatoes, peeled

vegetable oil, for frying

2 tbsp cornflour

1 tsp onion powder

1 tsp garlic powder

½ tsp salt

¼ tsp pepper

For the dipping sauce

5 tbsp mayonnaise

1 tbsp American classic yellow mustard (I like French's)

5cm piece of gherkin, drained and finely chopped

½ tbsp gherkin juice

1 tbsp tomato ketchup

¼ tsp garlic powder

¼ tsp onion powder

¼ tsp pepper

pinch of salt

Grate the potatoes into two different sizes (this creates a better texture). Place in a bowl and rinse until the water runs clear, then drain. Now place in a clean tea towel and squeeze all the moisture out. Half-fill a saucepan with vegetable oil and place over a medium heat until hot. Test with a small piece of bread – if it floats and bubbles, the oil is ready.

Now add the grated potatoes to the hot oil and cook for 5 minutes. Remove with a slotted spoon and drain on kitchen paper. Let the potato cool down (set the oil aside, too, away from the heat), then put into a bowl and add the cornflour, onion powder, garlic powder, salt and pepper. Mix well. Shape the mixture into hash browns (it makes eight) – I make little piles of the mixture, but you can shape it as you like. Place on a tray and refrigerate for 1 hour.

Mix all the dipping sauce ingredients together and put to one side.

Now cook the hash browns. Heat a tablespoon of the oil you used earlier in a frying pan until hot, then add the hash browns (you'll need to cook them in batches) and fry for 3-4 minutes on each side. They're done when they're nice and golden and crispy. Drain on kitchen paper and place on a wire rack while you cook the rest.

Put the hash browns onto a large serving plate with the dipping sauce alongside and dig in.

THE BIG MUSH 'UN!

SERVES 2

Nice and tasty alternative to sausage and bacon. Great for brunch or Valentine's Day or a birthday.

2 field mushrooms

2 tsp brown sauce

pinch of ground nutmeg

good splash of Worcestershire sauce

2 blocks of frozen spinach

1 tomato, cut into 4 slices

4 red onion rings

60g Cheddar cheese, sliced

2 eggs (the fresher the better)

salt and pepper

Preheat the oven to 180°C fan/200°C/gas mark 6.

Remove (and discard) the stalks from the mushrooms and place the mushrooms on a baking tray. Spread the brown sauce over the mushrooms and season with a pinch each of salt and pepper and the nutmeg. Splash some Worcestershire sauce over them. Set aside.

Cook the spinach according to the pack instructions, then run under cold water and squeeze all the moisture out. Spread the spinach over the mushrooms. Now place the tomato slices on top, followed by the onion rings, then the sliced cheese.

Bake in the oven for 30-35 minutes. The mushrooms are done when most of the moisture has gone and the cheese is nice and golden.

About 10 minutes before the mushrooms are ready, half-fill a saucepan with water. Bring to a low simmer. Use a spoon to swirl the water around (not too fast), then crack the eggs into the water, one at a time, and poach for 4-5 minutes. Check the eggs are done when you press the yolk and it's still runny inside, but the white is set. Remove with a slotted spoon and drain on kitchen paper.

Now place the mushrooms on plates and top with the poached eggs. Season the eggs with salt and pepper and enjoy.

 Use any hard cheese of your choice.

PRAWN AND CORN FRITTERS WITH ROASTED RED PEPPER SAUCE

SERVES 4–5 (MAKES 15–16 FRITTERS)

These fritters are completely moreish.

For the fritters

200g frozen peeled prawns, defrosted and roughly chopped

100g frozen sweetcorn, defrosted (or use canned)

2 tbsp chopped red onion

3 garlic cloves, crushed

2 tbsp chopped parsley

zest and juice of ½ lemon

4 tbsp plain flour

½ tsp baking powder

1 tbsp Dijon mustard

2 tsp paprika

½ tsp caster sugar

4 tbsp mayonnaise

1 egg, beaten

½ tsp salt

½ tsp pepper

For the sauce

1 red pepper, deseeded and cut into large chunks

¼ red onion, cut into large chunks

3 garlic cloves, peeled

¼ tsp dried thyme

100g cherry tomatoes

¼ tsp salt

¼ tsp pepper

¼ tsp cayenne pepper

pinch of caster sugar

To cook and serve

vegetable oil, for roasting and frying

few handfuls of rocket leaves, to serve

Preheat the oven to 180°C fan/200°C/gas mark 6.

In a bowl, mix together all the fritter ingredients and then put into the fridge.

Now mix together the sauce ingredients in an ovenproof dish, but leaving out the salt, pepper, cayenne and sugar. Coat with oil and roast in the oven for around 30 minutes. It's done when the peppers and tomatoes are blistered. Remove and cool for 15 minutes. When cooled, blend together in a blender or food processor and then add the salt, pepper, cayenne and sugar and mix again.

Now cover the bottom of a frying pan with some vegetable oil and place over a medium heat until hot. The oil is ready when it starts to bubble if you put a little bit of the fritter mix in. Using about 1 tablespoon of the mixture for each fritter, add a few dollops of the fritter mix to the pan (you'll need to cook the fritters in batches). Cook on one side until nice and golden, then flip over and cook until golden on the other side, about 4–6 minutes in total. Remove and drain on kitchen paper. Keep warm while you cook the rest in the same way, adding a little extra oil to the pan if needed.

To serve, place 3–4 fritters on each plate. Put a handful of rocket leaves next to the fritters, then spoon over the red pepper sauce.

TOMATO & GARLIC CONFIT

SERVES 2

You want the tomatoes to just start to blister but not turn to mush. Check the cooked garlic by pinching it - when it's done you should be able to spread it on your toast. Don't throw away the oil, save it for future use.

300g cherry tomatoes

10 garlic cloves, peeled

5-6 small shallots, quartered

2 tsp harissa paste

good pinch of caster sugar

olive oil, to cover

4 sprigs of thyme

4 slices of tiger loaf

1 x 300g tub cottage cheese

drizzle of balsamic vinegar

salt and pepper

Preheat the oven to 145°C fan/165°C/gas mark 3.

Place the tomatoes, garlic, shallots, harissa paste, sugar and a good pinch each of salt and pepper in an ovenproof dish (approx. 18 x 15 x 6cm) and toss to coat the tomatoes and shallots. Now add enough olive oil to just cover the tomatoes. Add your thyme sprigs and make sure they're submerged as well.

Bake in the oven for around 45-60 minutes, depending on the size of the tomatoes. Stir halfway through. It's ready when the tomatoes are blistering but still retain their shape, and the garlic is nice and tender - you should be able to spread it.

Remove from the oven and cool to room temperature, then cover and chill in the fridge until needed. It will last a few days in the fridge, covered (see Tip).

To serve, toast the bread, then place 2 slices on each plate. Take 8 garlic cloves out of the confit and spread on the toast, 2 cloves per slice. Now spoon as much or as little of the cottage cheese as you like on the toast (if you have any left over, it will keep in the fridge). Top with the tomato confit, making sure to put some of the cooking oil over as well (that's liquid gold). Season to taste and drizzle balsamic vinegar over the top.

 Take the confit out of the fridge and bring to room temperature before serving.

- FRITARTA
- ~~OVEN BAKED ITALIAN CHICKEN~~
- ~~HONEY GLAZED ROASTED CAULIFLOWER~~ CREAMED FETA / PINE NUT DRESSING ?
- ~~BLACK BEAN & VEGTABLE UDON NOODLES~~
- ~~GRILLED PORK CHOPS WITH SWEAT & SOUR~~ ✔ PEPPERS
- ~~GRILLED PORK CHOPS WITH SLAW & PEACH &~~ RUM SAUCE
- VEGTABLE PASTA BAKE
- LEFT OVER ROAST MEAT RAMEN
- PULLED PORK BURGER WITH CRACKING MAYO
- STICKY BOURBON GLAZED HAM + GAMMON
- PRAWN CURRY
- ~~PIMPED UP BUBBLE AND S~~
- PIMPED UP PIGS IN BLANKETS & ONION GRAVY ✔
- ONE POT WHOLE CHICKEN ✔ WITH ALL THE VEG / CIDER OR WHITE WINE
- LEMON PEPPER CHICKEN / GARLIC & HERB CRUSHED POTATOES / LEMON BUTTER SAUE ✔
- PORK CHOPS (?) AND POTATOE TRAY BAKE
- EASY PEASY SAUSAGE & CIDER STU ✔
- CHICKEN MARINATED IN CHIP SHOP CURRY ~~SOURE~~ SOURCE
- EASY CAULIFLOWER + COCONUT CURRY ✔
- CHICKEN IN BLACK BEAN
- NOODLE SALAD

PIMPED-UP PIGS IN BLANKETS WITH ONION GRAVY

SERVES 4

This is a great dish to use up leftovers during the period between Boxing Day and New Year's Day. Tasty. A great Crimbo idea.

8 Cumberland sausages

16 rashers smoked streaky bacon

2 tbsp cranberry sauce

1 tbsp wholegrain mustard

1 tbsp balsamic vinegar

1 tbsp vegetable oil

1 large onion, sliced

1 tsp caster sugar

1½ tsp plain flour

300ml chicken stock

1 tsp Worcestershire sauce

salt and pepper

To serve

Bubble and Squeak (see page 38)

2 handfuls of watercress

Preheat the oven to 180°C fan/200°C/gas mark 6.

Take your sausages and wrap each one in 2 bacon rashers, then put to one side.

Now mix the cranberry sauce, mustard and vinegar together in a small bowl. Mix well, then microwave on Low for 30 seconds to loosen. This is your glaze for the sausages.

Place the bacon-wrapped sausages on a baking tray or in a roasting tin and roast in the oven for 10 minutes. Take out of the oven and start basting with the glaze. Return to the oven and repeat the process every 8-10 minutes to build up a nice glaze (this should take around 30-40 minutes in total).

Meanwhile, heat the vegetable oil in a saucepan over a medium-low heat. Add the onion and sugar, with a good pinch each of salt and pepper, and cook the onion down to a nice golden sticky consistency, stirring from time to time, about 10-15 minutes. Stir in the flour, then gradually add the stock, a little at a time, and keep stirring. Now add the Worcestershire sauce, then reduce down to a nice sauce-like consistency, stirring occasionally, about 5-8 minutes.

Take the sausages out of the oven. Pile the bubble and squeak onto plates. Place two sausages per person on top of the bubble and squeak. Spoon over the onion gravy. Place a handful of watercress to the side of each plate and enjoy.

STEAKS WITH HOME-MADE PEPPERCORN & BRANDY SAUCE

SERVES 4

It's definitely worth the effort with this sauce, 'cos it really elevates the steaks to another level. Everybody deserves a treat from time to time. These steaks go great with chips and Balsamic Cherry Tomatoes (see page 138).

4 steaks (the best you can afford)

3 tsp vegetable oil

¼ onion, finely chopped

1 tbsp brandy

250ml beef stock

½ tbsp black peppercorns

200ml double cream

1 tsp wholegrain mustard

1 tsp Worcestershire sauce

salt and pepper

Place a heavy-based frying pan over a high heat. When it's smoking, rub each steak with ½ teaspoon of the vegetable oil and season with salt and pepper. Now cook your steaks to your liking, turning a few times. Transfer them to a plate, cover with foil and leave to rest.

Turn the heat down to low. Add the remaining oil and the onion to the pan and cook until translucent, about 5 minutes. Now add the brandy and cook off the alcohol, then add the stock and reduce it by half, about 5-8 minutes. Meanwhile, coarsely grind the peppercorns using a pestle and mortar.

When the stock has reduced, add the cream, coarsely ground pepper, mustard and Worcestershire sauce and season with salt to taste. Keep stirring and continue to cook down to the consistency of your liking. Pour the steak resting juices into the sauce.

Plate up your steaks, pour the sauce over and enjoy.

THE ALMIGHTY TOAD-IN-THE-HOLE

SERVES 2

What can I say about this. It's a British classic. Adding the garlic and thyme just takes it up a notch or two. I recommend making the batter mix in advance, even the day before. This will allow everything to calm down. Just give it a little stir before cooking the toad.

150g plain flour

½ tsp dried thyme

200ml milk

4 medium eggs, beaten

4 garlic cloves, chopped

3½ tbsp vegetable oil

8 sausages (of your choice)

salt and pepper

In a large bowl, combine the flour, thyme and a good pinch each of salt and pepper.

In a separate bowl, add the milk, eggs and garlic and give them a good mix.

Now slowly add the wet mix to the flour mix, stirring all the time until nice and smooth. Don't over-mix – a few lumps is fine. Cover and put to one side at room temperature for at least 4 hours or overnight in the fridge, if possible (bring it to room temperature before using).

When you are ready to cook, preheat the oven to 210°C fan/ 230°C/gas mark 8.

Add 3 tablespoons of the vegetable oil to an ovenproof dish (approx. 28 x 23 x 6cm). Place in the oven for 10 minutes to heat up the oil.

Meanwhile, add the remaining ½ tablespoon of oil to a frying pan over a medium-low heat. Add the sausages and brown on all sides, about 5 minutes. Set aside.

Now take the dish out of the oven. Be careful. Arrange the sausages in the dish. Take your batter mix, add ½ tablespoon of water and give it a gentle stir, then pour the batter into the dish around the sausages. Place back in the oven and cook for 25 minutes. Do not open the oven door until the time is up. When it's ready, it should be nice and golden with a good rise. Take out of the oven and leave to sit for 5 minutes, then serve.

This goes nicely with cooked vegetables and gravy of your choice.

TEA

GRILLED PORK CHOPS WITH SWEET & SOUR PEPPERS

SERVES 2

The sweet and sour peppers go so well with the griddled chops. This makes for an easy midweek idea.

2½ tsp vegetable oil

2 red or yellow peppers, deseeded and cut into strips

½ onion, diced

2 pork chops

salt and pepper

For the sauce

3 tbsp malt vinegar

2 tbsp honey

1 tsp Worcestershire sauce

¼ tsp ground cinnamon

¼ tsp chilli flakes

¼ tsp dried thyme or ½ tsp chopped thyme leaves

¼ tsp salt

¼ tsp pepper

Heat 1½ teaspoons of the vegetable oil in a frying pan over a high heat. Add the pepper strips and stir for a few minutes. When you have colour on the peppers, add the onion. Keep stirring for a few minutes, then turn the heat down to medium-low.

Mix all the sauce ingredients together in a bowl, then pour this over the peppers in the pan. Keep cooking and stirring until the sauce has reduced down and is nice and sticky, about 3-4 minutes. Set aside and keep warm.

Meanwhile, preheat a griddle pan over a high heat until smoking. Brush both sides of the chops with the remaining 1 teaspoon of oil and season with a pinch each of salt and pepper. Place the chops in the griddle pan and cook to your liking, turning them over halfway through. Plate the peppers up alongside the chops.

LEFTOVER TURKEY & LEEK PIE

SERVES 2-3

This tasty pie is great at Christmas for using up leftover roast turkey – it also works well with leftover cooked chicken.

3 tbsp unsalted butter

450g leeks, washed and sliced

¼ tsp salt, plus an extra good pinch

¼ tsp pepper, plus an extra good pinch

300g leftover cooked turkey, shredded

3 tbsp plain flour

100ml milk

150ml dry cider

100ml double cream

½ tbsp wholegrain mustard

100g frozen peas

1 x 375g pack ready-rolled puff pastry (1 sheet)

Place 1 tablespoon of the butter and 1 tablespoon of water in a saucepan and melt. Add the leeks and cook over a low heat until the leeks have softened, about 5 minutes. Add a good pinch each of salt and pepper. Add the turkey and give it a good mix. Put to one side.

In a separate saucepan, melt the remaining butter over a low-medium heat, then stir in the flour. Start adding the milk, bit by bit, and keep stirring. When the milk is incorporated, gradually add the cider, bit by bit. The sauce should be nice and creamy. Now stir in the cream, mustard, peas and the remaining ¼ teaspoon each of salt and pepper. Pour the sauce over the turkey/leek mix and stir well, then tip into an ovenproof dish or baking tin (approx. 23 x 18 x 5cm). Cool slightly, then put in the fridge for 30 minutes to firm up.

Preheat the oven to 180°C fan/200°C/gas mark 6.

Take the pie mix out of the fridge. Unroll the pastry sheet and cut it to a bit bigger than the size of the dish/tin. Place the pastry on top of the pie mix with an overlap on all sides, then push down around the edges with a fork so you have a tight fit on all sides. With a sharp knife, cut off the overhang (see Tip), then poke a hole in the middle of the pastry lid.

Bake in the oven for 25-30 minutes or until the pie is nice and golden and bubbling. Serve hot.

If you like, you could brush the pastry with beaten egg before putting it in the oven. Make cheese straws with the leftover pastry trimmings.

EASY COCONUT CAULIFLOWER CURRY

SERVES 3-4

There's something about coconut milk in a curry that makes it feel special. Goes so well with spices. Sweet and spicy.

1 cauliflower, around 850g

½ tbsp vegetable oil

1 onion, chopped

4 garlic cloves, minced

thumb-sized piece of fresh ginger, peeled and minced

1 tbsp medium curry powder

½ tsp ground coriander

½ tsp ground cumin

½ tsp chilli powder

½ tbsp tomato purée

2 tomatoes, chopped

1 x 400ml can coconut milk

1 bay leaf

1 tsp caster sugar

salt and pepper

Remove the central stalk from the cauliflower and break the florets into bite-sized pieces. Heat the vegetable oil in a high-sided saucepan over a medium heat until hot, then add the onion and sweat down for around 5 minutes.

Add the garlic and ginger and fry for another minute. Stir in the curry powder, coriander, cumin and chilli powder. Dry-fry for a minute, then add the tomato purée and cook out for 30 seconds. Add the chopped tomatoes, then stir and cook until they start to release their juices.

Now add the coconut milk and bay leaf and give it a good stir. Add the cauliflower florets. Bring to a simmer, then stir in the sugar and season with a good pinch each of salt and pepper. Simmer gently, stirring regularly, until reduced by half, about 20-25 minutes. It's ready when the cauliflower is just tender.

Remove the bay leaf, and serve with plain boiled rice or cooked rice of your choice.

LEMON PEPPER CHICKEN WITH LEMON BUTTER SAUCE

SERVES 4

You will get a pat on the back for this one. Very impressive but not too complex.

zest of 2 lemons

¼ tsp black peppercorns

¼ tsp flaky sea salt

4 medium skinless, boneless chicken breasts

1½ tbsp vegetable oil

½ onion, chopped

200ml chicken stock

juice of 1 lemon

2 tbsp butter

2 tsp cornflour

½ tbsp chopped parsley

salt and pepper

Garlic and Herb Crushed Potatoes (see page 145), to serve

Preheat the oven to 140°C fan/160°C/gas mark 3. Line a small baking tray and spread the lemon zest all over. Place in the oven to dry out (around 4-5 minutes). Keep an eye on it. When it's dry, place in a pestle and mortar along with the peppercorns and salt and grind to a coarse powder. Set aside.

Cut each chicken breast in half lengthways. Place between two sheets of baking paper and flatten slightly using the bottom of a heavy saucepan (or a rolling pin).

Heat 1 tablespoon of the vegetable oil in a frying pan over a medium heat. Add the chicken and cook for 4-5 minutes on each side until cooked through and golden. The internal temperature of the thickest part of the chicken should reach 74°C/165°F and the juices should run clear. Transfer the chicken to a baking tray or large plate and keep warm in a low oven while you make the sauce.

Add the remaining oil to a saucepan, add the onion and sweat down over a medium heat until translucent, about 5 minutes. Add the stock to the frying pan you cooked the chicken in and deglaze all the goodness from the bottom of the pan, then pour this over the onion. Allow the stock and onion to reduce slightly, then add the lemon juice and butter. Keep stirring.

Mix the cornflour with a little cold water to make a paste with the consistency of double cream. Stir into the sauce in stages to your desired consistency (you might not need all the cornflour mixture). Season to taste with salt and pepper. Now stir in the parsley. Take the chicken out of the oven.

Spoon some potatoes onto each plate. Place two pieces of chicken on top. Sprinkle some lemon pepper mix on top of the chicken, then spoon some sauce all around the plate and serve.

GRIDDLED HALLOUMI WITH WEDGE SALAD & CURRY DRESSING

SERVES 2

Iceberg lettuce is my favourite lettuce. Fresh and crispy. So underrated. It takes the curry dressing so, so well. Stands up to everything.

100ml vegetable oil, plus ½ tsp

½ white onion, sliced

¼ tsp salt, plus an extra pinch

¼ tsp pepper, plus an extra pinch

¼ tsp caster sugar, plus an extra pinch

4 tbsp mayonnaise

1 tsp mild curry powder

juice of ½ lemon

225g halloumi cheese, cut into 6 slabs

½ iceberg lettuce, cut in half

90g cherry tomatoes, quartered

¼ red onion, sliced

Put the 100ml of vegetable oil into a saucepan and set over a medium heat. After a few minutes, test the oil by dropping a piece of the white onion in. If it starts to bubble and floats to the top, it's ready.

Now put the rest of the white onion into the oil and stir. Cook until golden and crispy, up to 5 minutes, then remove from the oil using a slotted spoon or spider strainer and drain on kitchen paper (cool and re-use the oil another time, if desired). Season with a pinch each of salt, pepper and sugar. Put to one side.

Now, in a bowl, mix together the mayonnaise, curry powder, lemon juice, 1 teaspoon of water and the remaining ¼ teaspoon each of salt, pepper and sugar. Put to one side.

Preheat a griddle pan or frying pan over a medium-high heat. Mix the halloumi slabs with the remaining ½ teaspoon of oil. When the pan is smoking, add the halloumi and cook on one side until you get grill marks, then flip over to get more grill marks on the other side. Then it's done (this will only take a few minutes).

Plate up by putting a wedge of lettuce onto each plate. Arrange the tomatoes and red onion around the lettuce. Spoon some dressing over the salad veg. Now place 3 pieces of griddled halloumi around the lettuce on both plates. Spoon over more dressing and finish by sprinkling all over with the crispy onion. Enjoy.

JUICY JUICY ONE POT CHICKEN

SERVES 4-6

I used to make this all the time when I lived on my own. I would have enough to feed me for three days. And hardly any washing up - a bonus!

300g carrots, peeled and chopped

300g swede, peeled and chopped

1 onion, chopped

5 garlic cloves, crushed

1 bay leaf

1 medium oven-ready chicken, 1.2-1.5kg

500ml chicken stock

250ml dry cider

4-5 sprigs of thyme

1 tsp Worcestershire sauce

¼ tsp salt, plus extra for the chicken skin

¼ tsp pepper, plus extra for the chicken skin

Preheat the oven to 160°C fan/180°C/gas mark 4.

Place the carrots, swede, onion, garlic and bay leaf in a Dutch oven or a large casserole dish. Place the chicken on top. Pour the stock and cider all around the chicken, then add the thyme sprigs and tuck them in. Add the Worcestershire sauce and measured salt and pepper and give it a good stir. Season the chicken skin with salt and pepper.

Place the lid on and cook in the oven for 2 hours. If you like, 10-15 minutes before it's ready, take the lid off to give the skin some colour. The chicken is done when the internal temperature is 74°C/165°F, but I find 2 hours in the oven is about right. It will probably exceed that temperature, but don't worry, cooking it in a Dutch oven means you will definitely end up with one juicy bird.

Remove from the oven, take the chicken out, place it on a large plate, cover with foil and leave to rest for 10 minutes. While you rest the chicken, place the lid back on the Dutch oven and pop it back in the oven to keep warm. Remove the bay leaf and thyme stalks before serving.

Carve the chicken and place in bowls, then spoon the vegetables and stock over the chicken. Serve with crusty bread and butter.

Note that the stock is not thick when served, it's nice and clean-tasting.

FENNEL SALTED ROAST CHICKEN

This is such a simple way to pimp up your chicken with little effort at all. The fennel complements the juicy chicken meat; the salt and pepper crisps up the skin so well. Spot on.

1 tbsp fennel seeds

1 tbsp flaky sea salt

1 tsp black peppercorns

2 tsp garlic powder

2 tsp onion powder

1 tsp caster sugar

1 oven-ready chicken, around 1.9kg

½ tbsp American classic yellow mustard (I like French's)

Put the fennel seeds, salt, peppercorns, garlic powder, onion powder and sugar in a pestle and mortar and grind to a rough powder. Put to one side.

Now take your chicken. With a sharp knife, slice through the meat to the bone twice on each leg, and slice through the breast twice on each side (just enough to expose the flesh). Now rub the mustard all over the chicken. This will act as a binder for the rub mixture to stick to.

Rub the fennel salt all over the chicken and into the cuts you made, and also put some into the cavity. Put the chicken on a plate and refrigerate, uncovered, for a minimum of 3-4 hours (or better still, overnight).

On the day of cooking, preheat the oven to 180°C fan/200°C/gas mark 6.

Place the chicken in a roasting tin and roast in the oven for about 1½ hours, basting the chicken halfway through with the juices. The chicken is cooked when the internal temperature reaches 74°C/165°F when a meat thermometer is inserted into the thickest part of the meat and the juices run clear. If the skin starts to go dark, you can loosely cover the chicken with foil.

Remove from the oven and rest, covered in foil, for 10-15 minutes. Carve the chicken to serve. It goes well with vegetables and roast potatoes, or it's good served in nice crusty baguettes with salad.

NUTTY NOODLE SALAD

SERVES 2

This dish is so nice. When you take your first mouthful, it's a flavour sensation.
You won't want it to end. You can taste all the individual flavours. Awesome.

150g beansprouts

½ red pepper, deseeded and sliced

½ yellow pepper, deseeded and sliced

1 carrot, peeled and cut into matchsticks

150g red cabbage, shredded

6 spring onions, sliced

160g dried egg noodles

For the sauce

3 tbsp crunchy peanut butter

3 tbsp sriracha sauce

1 tbsp soy sauce

½ tbsp cider vinegar

½ tbsp honey

juice of 1 lime

1 garlic clove, crushed

½ tsp peeled and crushed fresh ginger

½ tsp sesame oil

½ tsp chilli flakes

¼ tsp salt

¼ tsp pepper

For the sauce, place the peanut butter in a suitable bowl and microwave on Medium for 30 seconds to loosen it up. Now add all the remaining sauce ingredients, plus 1 tablespoon of water. Give it all a good mix until nice and smooth, then set aside.

In a separate large bowl, add all the vegetables and mix together. Set to one side.

Now cook the noodles according to the pack instructions. Once cooked, drain and cool under cold running water for 30 seconds, then drain.

Mix half the sauce with the vegetables, then add the noodles and the rest of the sauce and mix well. Cover and refrigerate for 1-2 hours. Take out of the fridge 30 minutes before serving to bring up to room temperature.

This noodle salad is great on its own or you could serve it alongside some barbecued meat.

CHRISTMAS GAMMON (CRIMBO GAMBO)

SERVES 6-8

It's a must in our gaff to have a gammon joint at Christmas. Me and my son Toby love one, either with the turkey on Christmas Day or through the week after Christmas. It's so versatile - you can have it with pickles, or add leftovers to pies, or serve as gammon, egg and chips. This is Toby's favourite.

2kg gammon joint

450ml dry cider

1 onion, quartered

1 garlic bulb, cut in half horizontally

1 bay leaf

1 tsp black peppercorns

3 tbsp soft dark brown sugar

3 tbsp balsamic vinegar

2 tbsp English mustard

2 tbsp redcurrant jelly

1 tbsp wholegrain mustard

1 tbsp honey

½ tbsp hot sauce (I like Frank's Red Hot Sauce)

½ tsp pepper

pinch of salt

Soak the gammon joint in cold water overnight to remove some of the saltiness.

On the day of cooking, place the gammon in a large saucepan. Add the cider, onion, garlic, bay leaf and peppercorns. Cover with water and place over a medium-high heat. Bring to the boil, then reduce the heat to a gentle boil. You will notice some scum coming to the surface, just keep skimming it off periodically. You will have to top up with water from time to time, too. Gently boil the gammon until the internal temperature reaches 60°C/140°F (anywhere from 40 to 60 minutes). The internal temperature will rise more when the gammon finishes cooking in the oven.

Remove the gammon and put to one side to cool slightly. Don't throw away the stock - it makes a great pea and ham soup (see my recipe on page 100).

Preheat the oven to 180°C fan/200°C/gas mark 6. Line a baking tray or shallow roasting tin with foil.

Put the rest of the ingredients into a small saucepan to make the glaze. Mix well, then cook over a medium heat until reduced slightly, about 5 minutes.

Now take the gammon and remove the rind, leaving a nice fat layer. Criss-cross the fat with a sharp knife. Place the ham in the foil-lined baking tray/roasting tin and brush a layer of the glaze all over. Roast in the oven, and keep basting with the glaze every 5 minutes to build up a nice glaze. The gammon is done when the internal temperature is 68°C/155°F (this should take around 20-25 minutes).

Take the gammon out of the oven and leave it to rest for 10-15 minutes, covered in foil, before carving.

FIVE SPICE DUCK LEGS WITH A SESAME SALAD & CRISPY 'SEAWEED'

SERVES 2

This is a quacking pair of legs. You have the crispy duck skin and tender meat. The sesame salad cuts through the fattiness of the duck so perfectly. And adding the crispy seaweed gives it a restaurant vibe!

2 duck legs

1 tsp five spice powder

¾ tsp salt

¾ tsp pepper

150g red cabbage (or a mixture of red and green cabbage), shredded

4 large spring onions, sliced

120g beansprouts

2 tbsp olive oil

2 tbsp cider vinegar

2 tbsp soy sauce

2 tbsp honey

2 tsp sesame oil

½ tsp chilli flakes

½ tsp caster sugar

1 tbsp sesame seeds

½ x quantity Crispy 'Seaweed' (see page 154), to serve

Preheat the oven to 160°C fan/180°C/gas mark 4.

Take your duck legs and prick them all over with a cocktail stick. This helps to release the fat and get a crispy skin. Now mix together the five spice powder and ½ teaspoon each of the salt and pepper. Rub this all over the duck legs, top and bottom. Now place them in an ovenproof dish and cook in the oven for 1½ hours. Check and baste them from time to time. The skin should be nice and crisp when done.

Meanwhile, put your cabbage and spring onions into a bowl and set aside. Bring a saucepan of water to the boil, then add the beansprouts. Bring back to the boil, then drain and cool under cold running water for 30 seconds. Drain and add to the cabbage mixture and mix well.

Now in a separate bowl, add all the remaining ingredients, minus the sesame seeds and crispy seaweed. Give them all a good mix to emulsify. Set aside.

Put a frying pan over a low heat, add the sesame seeds and toast for a minute or two. Tip the toasted seeds into the dressing, give it a mix, then pour over the salad veg. Stir well to coat.

When the duck is ready, spoon the salad onto the middle of two plates. Take the duck out of the oven and shred the meat off the bone. Place on top of the salad and sprinkle over the crispy seaweed. Enjoy.

ME MAM'S BACON ROLY-POLY

SERVES 5-7

This is legendary. There were seven in our family: mam and dad and five of us kids. My dad worked 60 hours a week and my mam brought us up proper old-school. So she would do recipes like this one on a budget and stretch meals out. Serving this with the tomato soup is ingenious.

200g bacon bits (pre-diced, uncooked bacon – I like smoked)

1 onion, chopped

¼ tsp pepper

150g self-raising flour, plus extra for dusting

75g shredded vegetable suet

1 x 400g can tomato soup

100ml milk

mashed potato and vegetables such as steamed broccoli or green beans, to serve

Preheat the oven to 190°C fan/210°C/gas mark 6½ and line a baking tray with greaseproof paper.

Place the bacon bits in a cold dry frying pan. Cook over a medium-low heat to render out the fat. When the fat starts to come out, turn the heat up to medium and cook the bacon bits until golden and crisp, about 8 minutes in total. Remove with a slotted spoon to a plate and put to one side.

Now fry the onion in the bacon fat until it's nice and golden, about 5 minutes. Turn off the heat and return the bacon to the pan. Season with the pepper and stir well. There is no salt in this recipe as the bacon will be salty. Put to one side.

In a bowl, combine the flour and suet. Mix well, then start to add 8-10 tablespoons of water, a bit at a time. You might need more, but you don't want the dough too wet. It should be like a shortcrust pastry consistency. Now flour the work surface. Firm your mixture together and roll out into a rectangle, around 25 x 20cm and the thickness of a pound coin. Now spread the bacon and onion mixture all over, right to the edges, then roll up from a short edge. Some filling may come out of the sides; just push it back in and pinch the sides shut.

Transfer the roll to the lined baking tray, seam-side down, then cook in the oven for 30 minutes. It should be nice and golden when it's ready. Remove from the oven and put to one side to cool slightly. Now heat up the soup, then stir in the milk.

Serve the roly-poly with mashed potato and vegetables. Place the mash and veg on serving plates. Slice the roly-poly and place a portion on each serving of mash, then spoon/ladle the tomato soup all over. Heaven.

EASY PEASY CIDER AND SAUSAGE STEW

Great tasty winter warmer. Definitely cheers you up on a cold rainy day.

1½ tbsp vegetable oil, plus ½ tsp for the sausages

8 sausages (of your choice)

2 onions, chopped

250g carrots, peeled and chopped into small bite-sized pieces

250g swede, peeled and chopped into small bite-sized pieces

4 garlic cloves, crushed

½ tbsp tomato purée

1 tbsp plain flour

250ml dry cider

400ml chicken stock

1 bay leaf

1 tsp English mustard

1 tbsp apple sauce

1 eating apple, cored and chunky chopped

¼ tsp pepper

salt (optional)

mashed potato, to serve

Put ½ teaspoon of the vegetable oil in a large frying pan over a medium heat. Add the sausages and brown on all sides for around 5 minutes. Remove to a plate and set aside.

Pour the remaining 1½ tablespoons of oil into the pan. Add the onions, carrots and swede and cook over a medium heat until you start to get colour, about 10 minutes. Add the garlic and cook for a further minute, then add the tomato purée and cook out for 30 seconds. Now stir in the flour, then add the cider and keep stirring until there are no lumps. Now add the stock.

Return the sausages to the pan, then add the bay leaf, mustard and apple sauce. Cook over a medium heat for about 5-7 minutes until the sauce starts to reduce, stirring from time to time. Just before it's ready, stir in the apple and pepper. You don't want the apple to mush down (I like the apple to still have a bit of crunch). Check for salt, but you might not need any.

The stew is ready when the sausages are cooked, the vegetables are just tender and the sauce has thickened (you may have to top up with a little water, if it gets too thick). Remove the bay leaf and serve the stew over mashed potato.

THE ITALIAN STALLION SLOW COOKER BEEF SANDWICH

SERVES 4

I got the inspiration for this dish from seeing how the Americans do the Italian beef sandwich. Tender beef packed into a sub roll dipped into the amazing stock it's been cooked in, topped with sweet peppers and mozzarella. What a combo. Tasty as!

2 tbsp vegetable oil

1 onion, sliced

1 red pepper, deseeded and sliced into strips

1 yellow pepper, deseeded and sliced into strips

800g stewing beef, diced

1 tbsp plain flour

300ml beef stock

150g closed cup mushrooms, sliced

5 garlic cloves, chopped

1 tbsp Worcestershire sauce

½ tsp malt vinegar

1 bay leaf

1 tsp dried oregano

1 tsp dried basil

1 tsp caster sugar

½ tsp chilli flakes

¼ tsp salt

¼ tsp pepper

2 x 30cm baguettes, each cut in half widthways (across the middle)

1 x 250g bag grated mozzarella cheese

1 x 150g jar (drained weight) whole green hot chilli peppers, drained

Turn your slow cooker on to high.

Now add 1 tablespoon of the vegetable oil to a large frying pan over a medium heat, add the onion and peppers and cook until they start to colour, about 5 minutes. Transfer to the slow cooker.

In the same pan, heat the remaining vegetable oil over a medium-high heat. Toss the diced beef in the flour to coat all over and then add to the frying pan. Colour the beef all over (this will take about 5–8 minutes), then transfer to the slow cooker. You might need to do this in 2 batches.

Deglaze the frying pan with a little of the stock and pour into the slow cooker, along with the remaining stock. Now add the rest of the ingredients, minus the baguettes, mozzarella and jar of chilli peppers.

Put the lid on and cook for around 4 hours. It's done when the beef melts in your mouth. If it doesn't, just cook for a bit longer until it does.

When the beef is ready, remove the bay leaf. Preheat the grill to high.

Take the baguettes and slice each portion down the middle (lengthways), not all the way through, and then load them with the beef mixture. Make sure to get plenty of juice in them as well – the more the better. Now sprinkle over as much mozzarella as you like and place under a preheated grill until the cheese has melted. Top with the green hot chilli peppers. Tuck in and enjoy.

PRAWN COCKTAIL WITH CRISPY BACON

SERVES 4

This is a showstopper. We love to have this on Christmas day as a starter. The smokiness of the bacon just hits the spot with the sweetness of the prawns.

2 rashers smoked streaky bacon

150g cooked peeled prawns (defrosted, if frozen)

200g iceberg lettuce, shredded

1 tomato, diced

8cm piece of cucumber, diced

salt and pepper

For the sauce

1 egg

2 spring onions, sliced

7 tbsp mayonnaise

1½ tbsp tomato ketchup

½ tbsp malt vinegar

juice of ½ lemon

¼ tsp caster sugar

good pinch of cayenne pepper, plus extra to garnish

For the sauce, start by hard-boiling the egg for 8 minutes, then cool under cold running water for 5 minutes. Peel and finely chop the egg and put into a bowl. Stir in the spring onions, then put to one side.

Add the mayonnaise, ketchup, vinegar, lemon juice, sugar, cayenne pepper and a good pinch each of salt and pepper to another bowl and mix. Add to the egg mixture and stir to combine. Set aside.

Preheat the grill to high. Grill the bacon rashers, turning once, until nice and crispy, about 6-7 minutes. Put to one side to cool.

Assemble each cocktail by putting a spoonful of prawns into a wine glass, then a spoonful of the sauce, then some lettuce, tomato and cucumber. Season this layer with a pinch each of salt and pepper. Repeat twice, finishing with a layer of prawns and lettuce and a spoonful of sauce on top. Sprinkle the cocktail with a pinch of cayenne pepper. Cut a rasher of bacon in half down the middle and stick one piece on top of the cocktail like a flake on an ice cream. Repeat three times to make 4 cocktails in total.

 You could make and assemble these cocktails a few hours ahead and leave in the fridge until you are ready to serve. If assembling in advance, cook the bacon just before you serve.

POTATO & LEEK SOUP WITH GARLIC CROUTONS

SERVES 4-6

My mum used to do us home-made soup on a Tuesday with cheese and pickle on a crusty baguette to dip into the soup. Tasted so awesome.

For the soup

600g leeks, washed and chopped

30g unsalted butter

4 garlic cloves, chopped

700g potatoes, peeled and washed

700ml vegetable stock

1 bay leaf

½ tsp salt

½ tsp pepper

200ml double cream

2 tsp wholegrain mustard

For the garlic croutons

200g baguette

1 tbsp unsalted butter

3 tbsp vegetable oil

2 garlic cloves, crushed

50g mature Cheddar cheese, grated (optional)

salt and pepper

Line a baking tray with greaseproof paper.

First, make the soup. Place the leeks in a saucepan with the butter and cook over a low heat until the leeks start to soften, about 5 minutes. Add the garlic and cook for 1 minute. Add the potatoes, stock, bay leaf, salt and pepper. Stir and place the lid on. Bring to a simmer, then cook until the potatoes are tender, about 15-20 minutes.

Once cooked, put the soup to one side to cool, remove the bay leaf, then blitz with a stick blender to the consistency you like. Stir in the cream and mustard and set aside.

Preheat the oven to 180°C fan/200°C/gas mark 6.

Now make the garlic croutons. Cut your baguette into bite-sized pieces and put into a bowl. Put the butter, oil and garlic with some salt and pepper into a saucepan over a low heat. Melt the butter, then cook the garlic for 1 minute. Pour the garlic butter over the bread pieces, tossing them to coat well. Add the cheese, if using, and toss together.

Spread the bread pieces out on the lined baking tray, then bake in the oven for around 10 minutes until golden and crispy, turning once or twice, but do keep an eye on them. Remove from the oven and set aside, while you gently reheat the soup in a saucepan.

Serve the hot soup in bowls and serve the croutons in a separate bowl so people can help themselves.

MUSHROOM & CABBAGE NOODLE SOUP

SERVES 2

I had a look in the fridge. I had cabbage and mushrooms to use up, so came up with this. That's the name of the game - just see what needs to be used up.

½ tbsp vegetable oil

¼ onion, sliced

3 garlic cloves, crushed

thumb-sized piece of fresh ginger, peeled and minced

2 field mushrooms, peeled and chopped

700ml vegetable stock

150g white cabbage, chopped

1½ tbsp hoisin sauce

1 tbsp Worcestershire sauce

1 tbsp sweet chilli sauce

½ tbsp soy sauce

1 tsp sesame oil

¼ tsp malt vinegar

¼ tsp pepper

good pinch of salt

2 x 50g nests of dried egg noodles

Heat the vegetable oil in a saucepan over a medium heat, then add the onion and cook for 5 minutes. Just when it starts to colour, add the garlic and ginger and cook for 1 minute. Add the mushrooms and cook for 1-2 minutes.

Now add the stock and cabbage and cook for around 5 minutes, then add all the remaining ingredients, minus the noodles. Cook for another minute or two, then add the noodles and cook for around 4-5 minutes until the noodles are tender (I like my cabbage to still have a bit of crunch).

Divide the soup between two bowls and serve.

STORECUPBOARD TOMATO SOUP

SERVES 4

I am proud of this one as most of the ingredients are from the storecupboard. It goes to show you really can produce tasty food from your cupboard. You've just got to use your imagination and see where it takes you.

½ tbsp vegetable oil

½ onion, chopped

3 garlic cloves, finely chopped

½ tbsp tomato purée

3 x 400g cans chopped tomatoes

½ vegetable stock cube

200ml boiling water

2 tbsp tomato ketchup

½ tbsp Worcestershire sauce

1 tsp malt vinegar

1 tsp caster sugar

½ tsp dried basil

¼ tsp pepper

good pinch of salt

1 tbsp double cream

Heat the vegetable oil in a saucepan over a medium heat, then add the onion and cook for 5 minutes, stirring from time to time. Add the garlic and cook for 2 minutes, then add the tomato purée and cook for 30 seconds. Keep stirring. Now add the canned tomatoes and stir well.

Dissolve the stock cube in the boiling water and add to the saucepan. Now add the rest of the ingredients, reserving the cream. Give it a good stir and simmer over a low heat for 15 minutes.

Turn the heat off and blend the mixture with a stick blender until smooth (or to your desired consistency). Now stir in the cream.

Divide the soup between bowls and serve. I like to serve mine with a cheese and pickle sandwich made with crusty bread.

BANANA & CHEESE TOASTIE

SERVES 2

I love a toastie and this is one combo I cannot live without. Trust me, you are going to want to make this every day.

1 banana (around 170g), peeled and sliced

½ tsp sweet chilli sauce

¼ tsp caster sugar

good pinch of ground cinnamon

good pinch of ground nutmeg

4 slices of bread (of your choice)

butter, softened, for spreading

50g mature Cheddar cheese, grated

salt and pepper

In a bowl, mix together the banana, chilli sauce, sugar, cinnamon, nutmeg and a good pinch each of salt and pepper. Mush down to combine.

Turn the sandwich toaster/toastie maker on.

Now take 2 slices of bread and put them side by side on a chopping board. Spread each slice of bread with half the banana mixture. Place the remaining bread slices on top to make 2 sandwiches, and butter the top sides.

When the sandwich toaster is ready, take half the cheese and divide it into the bottom side of two plates/moulds of the sandwich toaster. Pick up each sandwich and place, butter-side down, on top of the cheese. Now butter the top side of each sandwich and place the remaining cheese on top.

Close the lid and leave to toast. The sandwiches will be ready when they're nice and golden. Transfer the toasties to plates and cool for a few minutes before serving. Tuck in and enjoy.

 If you don't have a sandwich maker, you can toast the sandwich in a frying pan over a medium heat. Make sure the cheese has melted and stuck to the bottom side before turning over.

CHICKEN IN BLACK BEAN

DIMPED UP PIGS IN BLANKETS / BUBLE & SQEEK

ONION GRAVY

HAM EGG & CHIPS WITH PINAPPLE.
HABANERO SAUCE

- POT ROASTED CHICKEN THIGHS

6 COTTAGE PIE

ROASP PORK WITH HOMEMADE APPLE SAUCE ✓

CRAB CAKES BURGER. / PRAW COCKTAL SAUCE

ROAST CHICKEN WITH LEAK SAUCE

ROAST TURKE CRIMBO STYLE WITH
BEST EVER PAN GRAVY —— DEFINATLY!

MUSHROOM STU COULD MAKE DAY BEFORE ✓
THEN REHEAT.

FISH PIE SERVE WITH WATERCRESS SALAD ✓

ROAST CHICKEN GARLIC & HERB WITH PAN
GRAVEY. ✓

BANGERS AND MASH WITH MUSHROOM GRAVEY

MUSHROOM & STROGANOH

POACHED HADDOCK AND CHICKEN

MUSHROOM STROGANOFF ✓

CORONATION EGG STUFFED CHICKEN
WRAPPED IN HONEY GLAZED BACON ✓

PEA & HAM SOUP WITH MINTED CROUTONS

SERVES 6

This is such a great way to use up leftover Christmas ham/gammon. The mint croutons give it an extra dimension. Mint and peas is a classic.

1 tbsp unsalted butter

1 onion, chopped

2 garlic cloves, chopped

2 potatoes, peeled and cut into chunks

1.5 litres stock from boiling a gammon (see Christmas Gammon on page 82), or use chicken stock

7 tbsp vegetable oil

2 tsp wholegrain mustard

3 tsp mint sauce

2 tsp caster sugar

½ tsp salt

½ tsp pepper

4 slices of thick-cut stale bread

500g frozen peas

350g leftover cooked gammon, shredded (see Christmas Gammon on page 82)

6 tsp double cream

Preheat the oven to 180°C fan/200°C/gas mark 6.

Place a saucepan over a medium heat. Add the butter and then the onion and cook until the onion starts to colour. Add the garlic and cook for 1–2 minutes, then add the potatoes and give it a stir. Now add the stock, then bring to a simmer and cook until the potatoes are tender, about 15–20 minutes.

While the potatoes are cooking, put the vegetable oil in a bowl and add the mustard, mint sauce, 1½ teaspoons of the sugar and ¼ teaspoon each of the salt and pepper. Give it a mix. Now rip up the bread into bite-sized pieces and add to the bowl, making sure all pieces of the bread are coated. Transfer to an ovenproof dish and spread out in a single layer, then bake in the oven for about 10 minutes. The croutons are done when they are golden and crunchy, but keep an eye on them.

Now when the potatoes are done, add the peas to the pan and bring back to the boil, then turn off the heat. Using a stick blender, blend until nice and smooth, then add the gammon. Blend again for a couple of seconds just to break down the gammon but not too much (you need some chunks). Season with the remaining ½ teaspoon of sugar and ¼ teaspoon each of salt and pepper.

Ladle the soup into bowls and stir 1 teaspoon of cream into each portion, then top with the crunchy croutons and serve.

GARLIC PRAWNS

This is a brilliant starter. So simple, but so, so nice.

5 tbsp olive oil

5 garlic cloves, chopped

2 tsp smoked paprika

¼ tsp chilli flakes

¼ tsp salt

good pinch of pepper

juice of 1 lemon

200g frozen cooked peeled
   prawns, defrosted

4 spring onions, sliced

1 tsp chopped parsley

loads of crusty bread and
   butter, to serve

Add the olive oil to a frying pan over a medium-high heat. Add the garlic and cook for a minute or two. When the garlic starts to colour, add the smoked paprika, chilli flakes, salt, pepper and lemon juice and stir.

Now add the prawns and spring onions to warm them through, about 2-3 minutes. Just before serving, stir through the parsley.

Spoon into bowls and serve with loads of crusty bread and butter to mop up all the lovely juices.

ROAST PORK & HOME-MADE APPLE SAUCE

SERVES 4 WITH LEFTOVERS, OR SERVES 6 WITH GENEROUS PORTIONS

This dish takes a little longer to make but is really worth it. It's one you'll come back to time and time again.

1.5kg pork shoulder

2 tsp fennel seeds

1½ tsp flaky sea salt

1½ tsp vegetable oil

1 onion, quartered

2 carrots, peeled and cut into chunks

5 garlic cloves, peeled

600g cooking apples

20g unsalted butter

1 tbsp caster sugar

¼ tsp ground cinnamon

good pinch of ground nutmeg

¼ tsp chilli flakes

salt and pepper

Pat the pork skin dry, place on a plate and refrigerate, uncovered, for around 6 hours or overnight. This dries out the skin. When you are ready to cook, preheat the oven to the highest setting.

Now put the fennel seeds and sea salt into a pestle and mortar and grind to a fine consistency. Rub all of the pork with the vegetable oil, then spread and rub the fennel spice mix all over.

Place the onion, carrots and garlic in an ovenproof dish or roasting tin and place the pork on top. Add enough water to the dish to cover the vegetables (around 2.5cm). Roast in the oven for 15 minutes, then turn the oven down to 180°C fan/200°C/gas mark 6 and roast for a further 1 hour 30 minutes until the pork is golden and the internal temperature is 63°C/145°F. Keep an eye on it as you will need to top up the water every so often.

Meanwhile, peel and core the apples and cut into bite-sized pieces. Melt the butter in a saucepan over a medium heat. Add in the apples, sugar and 1 tablespoon of water. Cook until the apples start to break down, about 5-8 minutes. Now add the cinnamon, nutmeg, chilli flakes and a good pinch each of salt and pepper. Keep adding water, a tablespoon at a time (you'll probably need about 4 more tablespoons), so it doesn't dry out. Cook until the sauce is the consistency of your liking. Put to one side and keep warm.

Remove the pork from the oven and rest, covered in foil, for 10-15 minutes. Carve into slices. Serve the pork with the apple sauce, the vegetables and some crispy roast potatoes.

tip

The apple sauce, once cooled, will keep in an airtight container in the fridge for up to a week. It can be enjoyed hot or cold (if serving hot, just reheat gently in a pan until warmed through).

GARLIC & HERB ROAST BUTTER CHICKEN WITH PAN GRAVY

SERVES 4

Pushing the garlic and herb butter under the chicken skin is a great way to not only add flavour, but to keep the meat nice and juicy. Use your imagination and put your spin on it. Happy days.

1 onion, quartered

5 garlic cloves, skin on, smashed

2 carrots, peeled and cut into chunks

3-4 sprigs of thyme

1 medium oven-ready chicken, around 1.5kg

boiling water, to cover

½ tbsp plain flour

salt and pepper

For the herb butter

60g unsalted butter, softened

4 garlic cloves, crushed

½ tsp chopped thyme leaves

1 tbsp chopped parsley

1 tsp chopped chives

zest of 1 lemon

Preheat the oven to 180°C fan/200°C/gas mark 6.

Place the onion, the 5 smashed garlic cloves, the carrots and thyme sprigs in a roasting tin. In a bowl, mix together the herb butter ingredients and a good pinch each of salt and pepper, then put to one side.

Now take your chicken and a spoon. At the top of the chicken breast on the big opening side, slide the spoon in between the skin and the flesh. Go all the way down on both breasts to form a pocket each side of the backbone. Spoon three-quarters of the garlic butter mix into both pockets, dividing it evenly, then spread and smooth down. Rub the remaining garlic butter all over the chicken and season the skin with a good pinch each of salt and pepper.

Place the chicken on top of the vegetables in the roasting tin. Just cover the bottom of the tin with boiling water (this stops the vegetables burning). Now place the chicken in the oven to cook. After 20 minutes, start to baste the chicken with the juices. Repeat this process every 15 minutes. The chicken should take around 1¼–1½ hours, depending on the size. The chicken is done when the internal temperature reaches 74°C/165°F and the juices run clear – check the thickest part of the breast and test with a meat thermometer.

Now take the chicken out of the roasting tin and place on a plate. Lightly cover with foil and put to one side to rest.

Place the roasting tin over a medium heat on the hob. Add the flour and mix well, scraping all the goodness off the bottom of the tin. Now stir in 200ml of water. Bring to a simmer, stirring, and smash the vegetables to release their flavour. Simmer for a few minutes, then strain into a saucepan, making sure you push hard on the vegetables and garlic to get all the flavour. Simmer the gravy over a medium heat until it's reduced to the consistency of your liking. Season with a good pinch each of salt and pepper and add any juices from the resting chicken (don't waste flavour).

Carve the chicken and serve with roast potatoes, cooked vegetables and cauliflower cheese (see my recipe on page 158). Spoon the gravy all over and enjoy.

I would highly recommend investing in a meat thermometer. You'll have juicy meat every time.

MUSHROOM STEW

SERVES 4

This is packed full of vegetables – so good for you. The mushrooms give it a meaty feel but without the meat.

600g closed cup mushrooms

4 tbsp vegetable oil

300g carrots, peeled and cut into small chunks

300g swede, peeled and cut into small chunks

1 onion, sliced

5 garlic cloves, chopped

1 tsp tomato purée

1 tbsp plain flour

700ml chicken or vegetable stock

1 tbsp tomato ketchup

1½ tsp Worcestershire sauce

1 tsp soy sauce

½ tsp balsamic vinegar

1½ tsp chopped thyme leaves

1 bay leaf

¼ tsp pepper

good pinch of salt

1 tbsp chopped parsley, to garnish

Clean the mushrooms and cut into quarters. Heat 2 tablespoons of the vegetable oil in a frying pan over a high heat. When the oil is smoking, add the mushrooms and stir, then press the mushrooms down, then stir. Repeat a few times. When the mushrooms have a nice golden colour (about 5–8 minutes), transfer them to a plate and put to one side.

Now add the remaining oil to the pan, then add the carrots and swede and cook over a medium heat until they start to colour, about 10 minutes. Add the onion and cook for 2–3 minutes, then add the garlic and cook for 1 minute. Stir in the tomato purée and cook for 30 seconds, then add the flour and give it a good mix. Gradually stir in the stock.

Now add the fried mushrooms and the rest of the ingredients to the pan, except the parsley garnish. Cook for around 30 minutes, stirring occasionally. The stew will be done when the vegetables are tender and the sauce has thickened.

Remove the bay leaf, sprinkle over the parsley and serve. This is great with mash.

FISH PIE

SERVES 4-6

Using frozen haddock and prawns makes this reasonably cheap. Some frozen haddock needs to be defrosted before cooking; check the packet guidelines. Adding the boiled eggs helps to bulk it out as well. So comforting.

200g frozen smoked haddock fillet

1 bay leaf

½ onion, cut in half

300ml milk

2 tbsp unsalted butter

2½ tbsp plain flour

50g frozen peas

handful of parsley, chopped

zest of ½ lemon

good pinch of ground nutmeg

3 hard-boiled eggs (see page 90), peeled

100g frozen cooked peeled prawns, defrosted

salt and pepper

For the mash

850g potatoes

1 tbsp unsalted butter

3 tbsp milk

½ tsp English mustard

70g mature Cheddar cheese, grated

Preheat the oven to 180°C fan/200°C/gas mark 6.

For the mash, peel and cut the potatoes into chunks. Rinse under cold water, then place in a saucepan. Cover with water, bring to the boil and cook until fork tender, about 8-10 minutes. Drain and leave to steam dry.

When the potatoes are dry, add the butter, milk, mustard, cheese and a pinch each of salt and pepper. Mash until you have no lumps. Put to one side.

Now place the haddock, bay leaf, onion and milk in a saucepan. Bring to just below boiling point, then take off the heat and let it stand for 5 minutes. Take the haddock out and transfer into an ovenproof dish (approx. 23 x 18 x 5cm). Remove the skin and cut the haddock into chunks.

Now strain the milk, reserving it for the sauce (discard the flavourings). Melt the butter in a clean saucepan over a medium-low heat. Stir in the flour and cook for a minute, then start to stir in the reserved milk, little and often. Keep stirring until you have a nice sauce consistency. Add the peas, parsley, lemon zest, nutmeg and 2 good pinches each of salt and pepper. Give it a good stir.

Pour some cheese sauce over the haddock. Slice the eggs and layer over the top, then add a bit more sauce. Scatter the prawns over, then pour over the last of the sauce. Spoon the mash all over in an even layer, then scuff up the surface with a fork.

Bake in the oven for around 30 minutes until golden brown and bubbling. Serve with a rocket salad.

MEXICAN-STYLE BRAISED PORK SHOULDER STEAKS

SERVES 4

Such an easy maintenance dish. Easy prep. Once in the oven, you're pretty much free to do anything for a few hours, and the smells coming from the oven are divine.

1 tbsp vegetable oil, plus 1 tsp

½ onion, cut into chunks

½ red pepper, deseeded and cut into chunks

½ yellow pepper, deseeded and cut into chunks

4 garlic cloves, chopped

1 x 400g can chopped tomatoes

1 x 200g can sweetcorn, drained

2 tbsp tomato ketchup

2 tsp honey

zest and juice of ½ lime

1 tbsp smoked paprika

2 tsp ground cumin

1 tsp ground coriander

½ tsp chilli powder

1 tsp dried oregano

¼ tsp salt

¼ tsp pepper

4 pork shoulder steaks, about 170g each

coriander, to garnish (optional)

Preheat the oven to 160°C fan/180°C/gas mark 4.

In a medium saucepan, heat the 1 tablespoon of vegetable oil over a medium heat. Add the onion and cook for 2 minutes, stirring. Now add the peppers and cook for another 3 minutes, then add the garlic and cook for 1 minute. Add the tomatoes and sweetcorn, then turn the heat down to low and stir. Now add the rest of the ingredients, except the pork and coriander, along with 50ml of water. Give it a good stir, then keep over a low heat while you brown the pork.

Heat the remaining 1 teaspoon of oil in a frying pan over a medium-high heat. Add the pork steaks and cook on one side for around 3 minutes, then turn and repeat. Once you have a good colour on both sides, take them out and place in an ovenproof dish – mine was 30 x 15 x 6cm, but a 20 x 20 x 5cm would work as well. Now pour the veg sauce all over the pork, making sure you have some under the pork and all the pork is covered.

Cover tightly with foil and bake in the oven for around 2–2¼ hours. Halfway through, take it out of the oven and stir, making sure the pork is still covered in sauce. It's done when the pork is almost falling apart and is melt-in-the-mouth. Garnish with coriander.

I serve mine with some simple boiled rice to soak up all the amazing sauce. Enjoy.

GRIDDLED PEAR & STILTON SALAD

SERVES 2

Pear and Stilton is always a great flavour combo. Adding the oaty biscuits not only elevates it to the next level, it adds different textures to your palate. This makes a great starter.

1 tbsp olive oil, plus 1 tsp

1 tbsp cider vinegar

½ tbsp honey

½ tbsp wholegrain mustard

1 ripe pear

2 handfuls of mixed salad leaves

2 spring onions, sliced

50g Stilton cheese

2 sweet and crunchy oat biscuits (I like Hobnobs), crumbled

salt and pepper

Make the dressing first. In a bowl, mix together the 1 tablespoon of olive oil, the vinegar, honey and mustard. Add a good pinch each of salt and pepper, mixing well to emulsify. Put to one side.

Now cut the pear in half. Take out the core with a melon baller, then cut each half into three lengthways. Place in a bowl and coat the pears with the remaining 1 teaspoon of oil.

Now heat a griddle pan or frying pan over a medium-high heat until hot. Place the pear slices in the pan and cook for around 5-8 minutes, turning occasionally. They are done when you start to get charring on both sides.

To serve, place a handful of salad leaves on each plate. Arrange the griddled/fried pears on top and sprinkle with the spring onions. Crumble the Stilton over. Spoon the dressing all over and around. Finish by sprinkling over the crumbled biscuits.

FAMILY FAVOURITE COTTAGE PIE

SERVES 4-6

This is total comfort food at its finest. My daughter Liv also makes a banging one. It's great on a cold winter's night.

½ tbsp vegetable oil

500g minced beef

1 onion, chopped

1 leek, chopped

1 celery stick, chopped

4 garlic cloves, chopped

1 tbsp tomato purée

600ml beef stock

200g carrots, peeled and grated

150g swede, peeled and grated

2 tbsp brown sauce

1½ tbsp Worcestershire sauce

¼ tsp dried thyme

½ tsp salt

½ tsp pepper

100g frozen peas

1.5kg potatoes

50g unsalted butter

6 tbsp milk

4 tbsp horseradish sauce

100g Red Leicester cheese, grated

Add the vegetable oil to a large frying pan over a medium-high heat. When the oil is smoking, add the minced beef. Don't move it for a minute or two. When you start to get colour on the bottom, turn it and leave again. Some liquid will be released from the beef. Let it evaporate. Now start breaking up the beef. When it's coloured all over, about 8-10 minutes, turn the heat down to medium.

Push the beef to one side, then add the onion and leek to the pan and keep stirring for a minute. Now add the celery and garlic and cook for 1 minute, then add the tomato purée and cook out for 30 seconds. Add the stock, carrots, swede, brown sauce, Worcestershire sauce, thyme and ¼ teaspoon each of the salt and pepper. Stir, then reduce the mixture down so that when you drag a spoon through the mixture it takes a second or two for the liquid to move back, about 10-15 minutes.

Now transfer the beef mixture to an ovenproof dish (approx. 28 x 23 x 6cm) and mix in the peas. Press the mixture down with a spatula and cool, then place in the fridge for around 1 hour to firm up. This will stop the mash from sinking when you put it on top.

Now peel and cut the potatoes into big bite-sized pieces and rinse under cold water. Place in a saucepan and cover with water. Bring to the boil and cook until the potatoes are nice and tender (when a knife has no resistance when you poke them), about 15-20 minutes.

Meanwhile, preheat the oven to 180°C fan/200°C/gas mark 6.

Drain the potatoes and put them back into the saucepan. Let them steam dry, then add the butter and milk and mash till nice and smooth. Add the horseradish and the remaining ¼ teaspoon each of salt and pepper and mix through.

Take the beef mixture out of the fridge and spoon the mash all over in an even layer, covering the beef mixture. With a fork, rough the mash up all over, then top with the grated cheese.

Bake in the oven for 30-40 minutes. The cottage pie is done when it's hot, bubbling and golden brown. Take out of the oven and let it sit for 10 minutes. To serve, spoon the cottage pie onto plates and serve with a mixed rocket and watercress salad.

You could even make this a day ahead for a dinner party. Stress-free. Just assemble the pie and keep in the fridge overnight, then bake as above until hot through.

CORNED BEEF & BAKED BEAN PIE

SERVES 3-4

This dish is pure nostalgia - it will always remind me of school dinners. It's cheap and easy, and a great one to prep in advance. Yummy. Kids would like this one, too.

900g potatoes, peeled and cut into bite-sized chunks

½ tbsp vegetable oil

½ onion, chopped

3 garlic cloves, chopped

1 x 340g can corned beef, chopped into bite-sized chunks

2 x 410g cans baked beans

1 tbsp Worcestershire sauce

1 tbsp tomato ketchup

1 tsp malt vinegar

1 tsp smoked paprika

½ tsp 'mild' hot sauce

¼ tsp caster sugar

3 tbsp milk

1 tbsp butter

100g mature Cheddar cheese, grated

½ tsp English mustard

salt and pepper

Rinse the potatoes under cold water, then drain and place in a saucepan. Cover with water and bring to the boil. Cook until tender, about 15-20 minutes, then drain and let them steam dry. Put to one side.

Meanwhile, add the vegetable oil to a saucepan over a medium heat. Add the onion and fry until golden (I want that nutty taste), about 5 minutes, then add the garlic and cook for 1 minute. Stir in the corned beef and cook for 1 minute, then add the baked beans and stir over a low heat until hot. Now add the Worcestershire sauce, ketchup, vinegar, smoked paprika, hot sauce, sugar, 2 tablespoons of water and a good pinch each of salt and pepper and stir to combine. Put to one side to cool.

Preheat the oven to 180°C fan/200°C/gas mark 6.

Transfer the corned beef mixture to an ovenproof dish (approx. 23 x 18 x 5cm).

Now the potatoes are dry, put them back over a low heat just to warm the bottom of the pan. Turn off the heat. Add the milk, butter, cheese, mustard and a pinch each of salt and pepper and mash until smooth. Spoon the mash evenly over the corned beef mixture and scuff up the surface with a fork.

Bake in the oven for 20-30 minutes until golden and bubbling. Tuck in and enjoy.

MUSHROOM STROGANOFF

SERVES 3-4

This is such a good version. Only using 4 tablespoons of double cream, it still packs a punch, but is healthier at the same time.

1 tbsp vegetable oil

200g closed cup mushrooms, quartered

½ large onion, chopped

4 garlic cloves, finely chopped

50g frozen peas

1 tbsp brown sauce

1 tbsp Worcestershire sauce

½ tbsp smoked paprika

½ tsp caster sugar

¼ tsp ground nutmeg

¼ tsp chilli flakes

¼ tsp dried thyme

¼ tsp salt

¼ tsp pepper

4 tbsp double cream

½ tbsp chopped parsley

cooked rice (of your choice), to serve

Add the vegetable oil to a frying pan over a medium-high heat. When it's smoking, add the mushrooms. Cook until they are starting to colour, around 5 minutes, stirring from time to time.

Lower the heat, then add the onion and cook for a further few minutes until the onion is colouring, stirring. Now add the garlic and cook for 1-2 minutes. Stir in 300ml of water and bring to a simmer. Add all the remaining ingredients, except the cream, parsley and rice. Bring back to a simmer and cook until reduced by half, about 5-8 minutes.

Add the cream, stirring all the time, and cook down to your desired consistency, then stir through the parsley.

You can serve this with cooked rice of your choice. Place the rice in bowls and spoon the stroganoff all over. Enjoy.

CORONATION EGG-STUFFED CHICKEN WRAPPED IN HONEY-GLAZED BACON

SERVES 2

This sounds an odd one, but believe you me it certainly works great with chips and salad!

2 eggs

2 tbsp mayonnaise

¼ red onion, chopped

40g mature Cheddar cheese, grated

2 tbsp mild curry powder, plus 1 tsp

¼ tsp chilli flakes

juice of ½ lemon

1 block of frozen spinach

2 skinless, boneless chicken breasts, about 250g each

½ tsp onion powder

½ tsp garlic powder

6 rashers smoked streaky bacon

2 tbsp runny honey

salt and pepper

Preheat the oven to 180°C fan/200°C/gas mark 6.

Put the eggs in a small pan, cover with water, bring to the boil and cook for 8 minutes. Drain, crack the eggs and place under cold running water for 5 minutes. Peel the eggs and put into a bowl, then chop finely with a knife and fork. Now add the mayonnaise, red onion, Cheddar, the 2 tablespoons of curry powder, the chilli flakes, lemon juice and a good pinch each of salt and pepper. Set aside.

Cook the spinach according to the pack instructions, then drain, cool under cold running water and drain again. Squeeze out all the moisture and add to the egg mixture. Mix well.

Now take each chicken breast, one at a time. Using a sharp knife, cut down the middle (lengthways) of each breast to make a pocket. Be careful not to cut all the way through. Divide the egg mixture between the pockets.

Now mix together the remaining 1 teaspoon of curry powder, the onion powder, garlic powder and a good pinch each of salt and pepper, then rub this all over the chicken. Take your bacon rashers and, with the back of a knife, stretch each rasher on a chopping board. Wrap 3 rashers of bacon around each stuffed chicken breast, making sure to cover the pockets. Place on a baking tray.

Roast the chicken in the oven for about 30-35 minutes, basting/brushing the chicken with the honey every 10 minutes. The chicken is done when it's nice and glazed and the internal temperature of the thickest part reaches 74°C/165°F on a meat thermometer.

Dig in and enjoy.

TURBO PORK STEW & CHEESY DUMPLINGS

SERVES 4

This name came from when I first moved out into my own house. I used to make this stew for my mates using a cheap cider which was called Turbo. It was like paint stripper. Not an apple in sight. My mates seemed to eat and like it, probably because we were all drunk. All the money in the world wouldn't change those memories. Great times with the lads.

2 tbsp vegetable oil

300g carrots, peeled and cut into chunks

300g swede, peeled and cut into chunks

300g parsnips, peeled and cut into chunks

1 onion, chopped

4 garlic cloves, chopped

700g pork shoulder steaks, cut into chunks

1½ tbsp plain flour

300ml chicken stock

400ml dry cider

1 bay leaf

2 tbsp brown sauce

½ tbsp Worcestershire sauce

½ tbsp wholegrain mustard

2 tsp chopped thyme leaves

½ tsp caster sugar

¼ tsp salt

¼ tsp pepper

For the cheesy dumplings

100g self-raising flour

50g shredded beef suet

¼ tsp salt

¼ tsp pepper

¼ tsp chilli flakes

70g Red Leicester cheese, grated

3 tbsp apple sauce

½ tbsp chopped chives

Preheat the oven to 170°C fan/190°C/gas mark 5.

Place 1 tablespoon of the vegetable oil in a large frying pan over a medium heat. Add the carrots, swede, parsnips and onion and cook until starting to colour, about 10 minutes. Add the garlic and cook for 1 minute. Transfer the veg to a Dutch oven (or a large casserole dish) and put to one side.

Add the pork and plain flour to a bowl and give it a mix, making sure all the pork is covered. Heat the remaining oil in the same frying pan over a high heat. Add the pork and brown on all sides, turning occasionally, about 5-8 minutes. You'll need to do this in two batches. Transfer the browned pork to the Dutch oven/casserole.

Using some of the stock, pour into the frying pan to deglaze, then pour this over the pork. Add the rest of the stock and the cider to the pork mixture and give it a stir. Now add the bay leaf, brown sauce, Worcestershire sauce, mustard, thyme, sugar, salt and pepper and stir. Place the lid on and bake in the oven for around 2 hours. Give it a stir halfway through. It's done when the meat is almost falling apart and is melt-in-your-mouth. Cook for a bit longer if it isn't quite ready.

About 30 minutes before the stew is ready, make the dumplings. Mix the self-raising flour with the suet in a bowl. Stir in the salt, pepper and chilli flakes, then add the cheese and apple sauce. Give it a good mix, then add the chives. Now start adding some water (you'll need about 5-6 tablespoons in total), a bit at a time. Keep mixing until you get a sticky dough. Divide and roll the dough into 8 even-sized balls, then 20 minutes before the stew is done, take the lid off the Dutch oven/casserole and place the dumplings on top with space between.

Put the lid back on and return to the oven for the remaining 20 minutes until risen and golden brown. For extra crispy dumplings, take the lid off 10 minutes after the dumplings have been added and return to the oven for the remaining 10 minutes.

Tuck in and enjoy. You could serve this with mashed potatoes or crusty bread, if you like.

CHEESY PEASY PASTA PEPPERS

SERVES 4-6

A great idea, this one. It's a good way to get the kids involved, and if they have their mates around, they can all get stuck in making this.

3 large peppers (any colour)

½ tbsp vegetable oil, plus 1 tsp

1 onion, cut into 6 round slices; leftover onion chopped for sauce

1 tsp tomato purée

200g canned tomatoes

1 tbsp tomato ketchup

½ tsp garlic powder

¼ tsp dried basil

¼ tsp chilli flakes

¼ tsp salt

¼ tsp pepper

50g frozen peas

50g dried macaroni

150g Cheddar cheese, grated

Preheat the oven to 180°C fan/200°C/gas mark 6.

Chop the bottom and top off each pepper, then cut each pepper in half widthways like an onion ring and clean out the seeds, so you have 6 hollow pepper halves in total. Set to one side. Chop up the pepper tops and bottoms.

Heat the ½ tablespoon of vegetable oil in a saucepan over a medium heat. Add the chopped onion and chopped peppers and cook for around 5 minutes, stirring. Stir in the tomato purée and cook out for 30 seconds. Now add the canned tomatoes, ketchup, garlic powder, dried basil, chilli flakes, salt and pepper and cook for another 5 minutes. Turn the heat off and stir in the peas.

Meanwhile, cook the macaroni according to the pack instructions, then drain.

Oil a baking tray with the remaining 1 teaspoon of oil. Place the hollowed pepper halves on the oiled tray. Put a round of onion at the bottom of each one, then top with a small handful of the cheese (save the rest for later). Mix the pasta with the sauce and fill each pepper half with the mix.

Bake in the oven for 10 minutes. Meanwhile, preheat the grill to high.

Take the peppers out of the oven and top with the rest of the cheese, then place under the hot grill. They are done when the cheese is golden and bubbling. Serve with a salad.

COMFORT FOOD – OVEN-BAKED FRITTATA

Such a versatile dish, hot or cold, and it's great for a picnic. Cooking it in the oven is more user-friendly than doing it on the hob, too.

3 potatoes, peeled and halved

1½ tbsp vegetable oil

1 red pepper, deseeded and sliced

1 yellow pepper, deseeded and sliced

1 orange pepper, deseeded and sliced

1½ onions, sliced

4 garlic cloves, finely chopped

3 blocks of frozen spinach

10 medium eggs

200ml milk

150ml double cream

100g mozzarella cheese, grated

70g mature Cheddar cheese, grated

2 tbsp chopped parsley

½ tsp salt

½ tsp pepper

100g frozen peas

knob of butter

salad, to serve

For the honey mustard vinaigrette

3 tbsp olive oil

3 tbsp cider vinegar

1 tbsp honey

1 tbsp Dijon mustard

¼ tsp chilli flakes

salt and pepper

Preheat the oven to 180°C fan/200°C/gas mark 6.

Place the potatoes in a saucepan and cover with water. Bring to the boil and cook until just tender all the way through, about 10 minutes. Drain and let them steam dry. Put to one side.

Now put the vegetable oil into a frying pan or wok over a high heat. Add all the peppers and the onions and cook/stir-fry until they are starting to colour, about 5 minutes. Add the garlic and cook/stir-fry for another 2–3 minutes. Take off the heat and put to one side.

Now slice your potatoes and mix them through the peppers and onions. Cook the spinach according to the pack instructions, then drain, rinse under cold water for 30 seconds, drain again and squeeze all the water out. Tear up the spinach and stir it through the vegetable mix.

In a bowl, add the eggs, milk, cream, both cheeses, the parsley, salt and pepper and mix until well combined. Stir in the peas.

Now take your butter and grease a 28 x 23 x 6cm baking dish. Spoon half your pepper mix into it, then pour half your egg mix over. Repeat again.

Bake the frittata in the oven for around 40-50 minutes. During baking, once you have a nice colour on it, cover with foil for the remaining time.

While the frittata is baking, make the honey mustard vinaigrette. Put all the ingredients into a small bowl, add a pinch each of salt and pepper and mix until emulsified. Set aside.

Remove the cooked frittata from the oven and set aside to cool slightly before slicing to serve. Serve with salad and the honey mustard vinaigrette drizzled over.

LASAGNE OUR WAY

SERVES 6

This is such a crowd-pleaser in our gaff. We all love this one. It's very rare that we have leftovers as it's so good.

1 tbsp vegetable oil

1kg minced beef

2 onions, chopped

4 garlic cloves, chopped

2 x 400g cans chopped tomatoes

500ml beef stock

2 tbsp Worcestershire sauce

2 tbsp tomato ketchup

1 tbsp balsamic vinegar

½ tsp salt

½ tsp pepper

2 tsp dried basil

1½ tsp dried oregano

13 dried lasagne sheets

200g mozzarella cheese, grated

2 tomatoes, sliced

good pinch of cayenne pepper

For the cheese sauce

3 tbsp unsalted butter

3 tbsp plain flour

400ml milk

70g mature Cheddar cheese, grated

¼ tsp ground nutmeg

salt and pepper

Heat the vegetable oil in a large frying pan or saucepan over a high heat. When the oil is smoking, add the minced beef. Press down but do not stir. You want to get great colour. Once you start to see colour, stir once and repeat until the meat is browned all over, about 5–8 minutes. This is what gives it depth of flavour. You may have to spoon some of the fat out, if it's too fatty.

Now add the onions and cook for a minute or two, then add the garlic and cook for another minute or two. Stir in the canned tomatoes, beef stock, Worcestershire sauce, ketchup, balsamic vinegar, salt, pepper and dried basil and oregano. Turn the heat down and simmer until it's reduced but not too dry. When you drag a spoon through the mixture, you should be able to see the bottom of the pan for a second before the mixture falls back (about 10–15 minutes).

While the meat is cooking, make your cheese sauce. Melt the butter in a saucepan over a low heat, then stir in the flour. Cook for a minute, then start adding the milk, a bit at a time, and keep stirring. When all the milk is added, you should have a nice smooth sauce. Now stir in the Cheddar and nutmeg, followed by a good pinch each of salt and pepper.

Meanwhile, preheat the oven to 180°C fan/200°C/gas mark 6.

To assemble the lasagne, spoon a thin layer of the meat mixture into an ovenproof dish (approx. 28 x 23 x 6cm). Add a layer of the lasagne sheets (there will be 4 layers of lasagne sheets in total), butted up (do not overlap them). Now add a layer of meat (about a third of the meat) to cover all the pasta, then spoon a third of the cheese sauce over, followed by half the mozzarella. Add more lasagne sheets, followed by more meat and half of the remaining cheese sauce. Add another layer of lasagne sheets, then a final layer of the remaining meat. Now add one more final layer of lasagne sheets and cover with the remaining cheese sauce, making sure all the pasta is covered. Sprinkle the rest of the mozzarella on top. Arrange the tomato slices on top, then sprinkle over the cayenne pepper.

Bake in the oven for around 30–40 minutes. The lasagne is cooked when it's golden and bubbling. Take the lasagne out of the oven and let it sit for 20 minutes before serving. Serve with salad, drizzled with vinaigrette.

When assembling the lasagne, if the cheese sauce has gone thick, put it back over the heat, add a splash more milk and warm it through.

THE NOODLE LOVER BLACK BEANS WITH UDON NOODLES

SERVES 2

This is a great one if you love your noodles - there is something so satisfying about a big bowl of juicy noodles, especially udon noodles. I would advise purchasing the fermented black beans from an Asian or Chinese supermarket. Trust me, you will thank me later. They last forever in the cupboard as well, so it's money well spent.

3 tbsp fermented black beans

4 x 150g packs pre-cooked udon noodles

boiling water, to cover

4 tbsp soy sauce

2 tbsp oyster sauce

1 tbsp hoisin sauce

1 tsp sesame oil

1 tsp Shaoxing wine

1 tsp caster sugar

¼ tsp salt

¼ tsp pepper

¼ tsp chilli flakes

1 tbsp cornflour

1 tbsp vegetable oil

½ onion, cut into chunks

½ red pepper, deseeded and cut into chunks

½ green pepper, deseeded and cut into chunks

4 garlic cloves, chopped

½ tsp peeled and chopped fresh ginger

A handful of beansprouts

Rinse the black beans in water, drain, then slightly crush them. Put to one side.

Put the noodles into a heatproof bowl and add enough boiling water to cover. Leave for a minute, then start to separate them. Drain and put to one side.

Now mix together the soy sauce, oyster sauce, hoisin sauce, sesame oil, Shaoxing wine, sugar, salt, pepper and chilli flakes in a bowl. Blend the cornflour with 50ml of water in a cup, then add it to the sauce bowl along with another 50ml of water. Give it a good mix.

Heat the vegetable oil in a wok or frying pan over a medium-high heat. When it starts to smoke, add the onion and peppers. Keep stirring. When you start to get colour, after about 5 minutes, turn the heat down, add the garlic and ginger and fry for a minute. Add the black beans and fry for another minute. Keep stirring. Now add the beansprouts and stir-fry for 1 more minute. Add the sauce mixture to the pan and stir-fry until the sauce has reduced and thickened, about 2-3 minutes. Fold in the noodles and stir-fry for another minute or two. The noodles should all be coated with the sauce clinging to them.

Spoon into bowls and dig in.

- LEEK SAUCE
- BALSAMIC TOMATOES ✓
- MAC & CHEESE
- SMASHED CUCUMBER SALAD ✓
- ROSEMARY/GARLIC & ORANGE ROASTED CARROTS ✓
- ~~PRAWN COCKTAIL / WITH CADDIE SMOKED STREAKY BACON~~
- PRAWN TOAST (WITH CARAMLISED ONIONS MIX IN ?)
- STUFFED MUSHROOMS (TO BE DECIDED)
- SPICED BRAISED RED CABBAGE
- BEER BATTERED ONION RINGS WITH DIPPING SAUCE
- PEAR & APPLE SLAW ✓
- MINI TORD IN THE HOLES WITH A TWIST.
- ~~CHICKEN FRIED~~ RICE COCONUT RICE
- BOMBAY POTATOES ✓
- ULTIMATE CHICKEN GRAVY MADE FROM PAN DRIPPINGS & VEG A GRAVY CAN MAKE OR BREAK A MEAL
- MANGO SALSA. ✓
- DONNAS STILTON SPUDS (DEFINETLY) ✓
- CAULIFLOWER CHEESE ✓
- GARLIC & HERB CRUSHED POTATOES ✓

SNACKS
SIDES

SMASHED CUCUMBER SALAD

SERVES 2-3

This is a great starter or side for an Asian-inspired dinner party. So fresh and clean tasting. Any leftovers will keep in the fridge for 3-4 days.

1 cucumber, around 400g

1 tsp salt

1 garlic clove, crushed

½ tsp chilli flakes

1 tsp sesame seeds

1 tbsp vegetable oil

½ tbsp malt vinegar

½ tsp sesame oil

1 tbsp honey

2 spring onions, sliced

Peel the cucumber in staggered intervals lengthways (to give a stripy effect). Place on a chopping board and smash with a rolling pin, not too hard - you just want to see some splits. Cut the cucumber in half lengthways, then cut the 2 halves down the middle again. You end up with 4 pieces of cucumber. Now chop them into bite-sized chunks. Put the cucumber chunks in a bowl and sprinkle the salt over, then set aside for 10 minutes. This will draw the excess moisture out of the cucumber. After 10 minutes, rinse under cold water, drain well and put back in the bowl.

Meanwhile, put the garlic, chilli flakes and sesame seeds in an ovenproof dish. Heat the vegetable oil in a saucepan over a high heat until it just starts to smoke (be careful). Pour the hot oil over the garlic mixture. It will start to bubble, but don't worry. It almost takes the edge off the raw garlic. Now stir in the vinegar, sesame oil and honey, then pour this over the cucumber. Add the spring onions to the cucumber and dressing and mix to combine.

Cover and chill in the fridge for a couple of hours to allow the flavours to build before serving.

BALSAMIC CHERRY TOMATOES

SERVES 2-3

Me and Don have been doing these since I can remember. They're like a flavour bomb in your mouth. The trick is to get them to just start to blister and stay in shape. These go well with steak, chips and salad.

300g cherry tomatoes

1 tsp olive oil or vegetable oil

handful of basil, torn

½ tsp caster sugar

2 tbsp balsamic vinegar (see Tip)

juice of ½ lemon

salt and pepper

Place the tomatoes in a saucepan, drizzle with the oil and stir. Turn the heat to medium and cook the tomatoes, stirring occasionally, until they start to blister, about 3-4 minutes. Season with a good pinch each of salt and pepper. Keep stirring.

Now stir in the basil, then add the sugar and balsamic vinegar. Keep stirring until the balsamic has reduced down to a nice sticky consistency.

Squeeze in the lemon juice and stir. Remove from the heat and let it cool slightly so the tomatoes firm up a little before serving. This is nice hot or cold.

You can use cheap balsamic vinegar for this, you don't need to buy an expensive bottle.

ORANGE HONEY BUTTER CARROTS

SERVES 2-3

These glazed carrots go great with ya roast dinner. It mixes it up a bit.

600g carrots

2 tbsp unsalted butter

2 tbsp honey

zest and juice of ½ orange

½ tsp malt vinegar

good pinch of ground nutmeg

1 tsp chopped thyme leaves or ¼ tsp dried thyme

salt and pepper

1-2 spring onions, chopped, to garnish

Peel the carrots and cut in half lengthways, then cut into bite-sized chunks. Place in a saucepan, cover with water and bring to the boil, then cook until just tender, about 5 minutes.

Meanwhile, place the butter in a frying pan over a medium heat. Let it melt, then add the honey and stir. Next, add the orange zest and juice, vinegar, nutmeg and a pinch each of salt and pepper. Keep cooking and stirring until it's reduced down to a sticky syrup consistency.

Add the thyme. Drain the carrots and add them to the sauce. Give them a good stir to cover them in the sauce. Tip the carrots into a serving dish and garnish with the spring onions.

PEAR & APPLE SLAW

SERVES 6

Can't think of a better dish to get your 5 a day in. So good for you. The dressing just coats the veg like you're dressing pasta. I don't like the slaw dripping in too much dressing.

5 tbsp mayonnaise

2 tbsp salad cream

juice of ½ lemon

½ tsp English mustard

1 tsp honey

½ tsp salt

½ tsp pepper

300g white or red cabbage, shredded

150g carrots, peeled and grated

½ red onion, chopped

1 eating apple, cored and cut into small chunks

1 ripe pear, cored and cut into small chunks

In a bowl, mix together the mayonnaise, salad cream, lemon juice, mustard, honey, salt (see Tip) and pepper. Put the shredded cabbage and grated carrots into another bowl. Add the onion, apple and pear and stir. Finally, spoon over the mayo dressing and mix well, then serve. This slaw is great for a family barbecue.

 Add the salt just before serving, if not eating the slaw immediately, otherwise the salt will draw moisture out of the vegetables and the dressing will go runny.

BOMBAY ROAST POTATOES

SERVES 4

When roasting potatoes in the oven, I find I can get them nice and crispy without using too much oil. These go so well if you're having a curry night.

1kg potatoes, skin on, cut into bite-sized chunks

1½ tsp ground turmeric

4½ tbsp vegetable oil

½ onion, chopped

3 garlic cloves, crushed

thumb-sized piece of fresh ginger, peeled and minced

1 tsp medium curry powder

½ tsp ground cumin

½ tsp ground coriander

½ tsp paprika

½ tsp chilli powder

½ tbsp tomato purée

2 tomatoes, chopped

½ tsp malt vinegar

½ tsp caster sugar

½ tsp salt

¼ tsp pepper

chopped coriander, to garnish (optional)

Preheat the oven to 180°C fan/200°C/gas mark 6.

Rinse the potatoes under cold water, then drain, place in a saucepan and cover with water. Add 1 teaspoon of the turmeric - this adds colour to the potatoes. Bring to the boil, then cook until only just tender, about 8 minutes (you only want to parboil them). Drain and let them steam dry.

Pour 4 tablespoons of the vegetable oil into a roasting tin and place in the oven to heat up. When the potatoes are dry, add to the oil and stir to coat in the oil. Roast in the oven for about 35-40 minutes until they are really crispy, turning once or twice.

Meanwhile, add the remaining ½ tablespoon of oil to a frying pan and fry the onion over a medium heat until you get some colour, about 6-7 minutes. Add the garlic and ginger and fry for 1 minute, then add all the ground spices (including the remaining ½ teaspoon of turmeric) and fry for another minute. Stir in the tomato purée and cook it out for 1 minute, then add the chopped tomatoes followed by 100ml of water, the vinegar, sugar, salt and pepper. Continue to cook, stirring occasionally, until the sauce is reduced down to a curry-like consistency, about 8-10 minutes.

When the potatoes are done, tip them into a serving bowl and cover with the curry sauce, then garnish with some chopped coriander, if you like.

GARLIC & HERB CRUSHED POTATOES

SERVES 4

Garlic and herbs with sautéed potatoes. What more can I say. Yummy. Great side for any dinner party.

800g potatoes, skin on, cut into bite-sized chunks

about 2 tbsp vegetable oil

4 garlic cloves, finely chopped

2 tsp chopped thyme leaves

2 tsp chopped rosemary

salt and pepper

Rinse the potatoes under cold water, then drain, place in a saucepan and cover with water. Add a pinch of salt and bring to the boil, then parboil until just tender, about 8 minutes. Drain and let them steam dry.

Add the vegetable oil to a frying pan and set over a medium heat. Add the potatoes and sauté, stirring from time to time. When they start to get some colour (after 7–8 minutes), crush them slightly with a spatula. Keep stirring for 3 minutes. Before they are done, add the garlic and herbs, stirring all the time. You may need to add a little more oil. When the potatoes are nice and golden (after about 5–8 minutes), season to taste with salt and pepper, then serve.

DON'S FAVE STILTON SPUDS

These were a real surprise after doing them on TV. I had such a response - from people on social media cooking them and tagging me, to being featured in *Delicious* magazine and the Saturday *Times*. Obviously by the name, Don absolutely loves them. Definitely advise you to do this at your next get-together. You'll gain friends for life.

850g potatoes

½ tsp salt

2-3 tbsp vegetable oil

220g Stilton cheese

¼ tsp pepper

3 spring onions, sliced

1 tsp chilli flakes

Preheat the oven to 180°C fan/200°C/gas mark 6.

Peel the potatoes and cut into the size you like your roast potatoes. Rinse under cold water and drain, then place in a saucepan, cover with water and add the salt. Bring to the boil over a high heat, then turn the heat down to a rolling boil and cook until tender, about 8-10 minutes. Drain and let them steam dry.

Now add the vegetable oil to a roasting tin and place in the oven for 5 minutes to heat up. Shake your potatoes in their pan to rough them up around the edges. Remove the roasting tin from the oven and add the potatoes. Turn to coat them all in the oil, then return to the oven and roast for 15 minutes. Take the potatoes out and give them a stir, then return to the oven for another 10 minutes or so - they should be starting to colour. Remove from the oven.

Crumble the Stilton all over the potatoes and put them back in the oven to roast until the Stilton is gooey and crispy, about 20 minutes. Remove from the oven and season with the pepper. You probably won't need salt as the Stilton is salty.

Garnish with the spring onions and chilli flakes and tuck in.

SWEET POTATO CHIPS WITH BLUE CHEESE DIPPING SAUCE

SERVES 2 FOR SHARING

The sweetness from the potato goes so well with the strong tangy flavour of the Stilton and all the rest of the ingredients in the dipping sauce. Nice little appetiser.

750g sweet potatoes

2 tbsp cornflour

4 tbsp vegetable oil

1 tsp smoked paprika

1 tsp onion powder

1 tsp garlic powder

1 tsp cayenne pepper

¼ tsp salt, plus a good pinch

¼ tsp pepper, plus a good pinch

mixed salad, to serve (optional)

For the sauce

5 tbsp Greek yogurt

2 tbsp soured cream

2 spring onions, finely chopped

zest and juice of ½ lemon

¼ tsp caster sugar

150g Stilton cheese

Preheat the oven to 180°C fan/200°C/gas mark 6.

Peel and cut the sweet potatoes into chips. Place in a large food bag with the cornflour and shake to cover all the chips. Now add the vegetable oil and shake again. Add the smoked paprika, onion powder, garlic powder, cayenne pepper and ¼ teaspoon each of the salt and pepper and shake again. Tip into an ovenproof dish or roasting tin and spread out in a single layer, then roast in the oven for 30 minutes. Take the tin out of the oven and turn the chips. Return to the oven and roast for a further 20 minutes or so. The chips are cooked when they are nice and brown, almost starting to burn.

While the chips are cooking, make the dipping sauce by putting the yogurt, soured cream, spring onions, lemon zest and juice, sugar and the pinch each of salt and pepper into a bowl. Mix well. Now crumble in the Stilton, then mash the Stilton down a bit with a fork and stir well.

To serve, transfer the chips to a large plate with the dipping sauce alongside and dig in. You could serve this with a mixed salad as well, if you like. Enjoy.

CHIP SHOP CURRY SAUCE & CHIPS

SERVES 4 WITH PLENTY OF SAUCE FOR EACH ONE

Who doesn't like curry sauce and chips from the chip shop? I certainly do. Can't get enough of it. So we make our own, enough to have plenty. Me, Donna and the kids love it! This goes nicely with sausages, roast chicken and fish.

1kg potatoes

2 tbsp vegetable oil

2 tbsp medium curry powder

½ tsp ground turmeric

½ tsp pepper

¼ tsp ground cinnamon

¼ tsp ground ginger

1 onion, chopped

3 garlic cloves, chopped

2 medium eating apples, peeled, cored and chopped

1 tbsp plain flour

500ml chicken or vegetable stock

1 tsp malt vinegar

1 tsp Worcestershire sauce

1 tsp caster sugar

a squeeze of orange juice (optional)

1-2 tbsp raisins (optional)

salt

Preheat the oven to 180°C fan/200°C/gas mark 6.

Peel, then cut the potatoes into chips. Rinse under cold water, then place the potatoes in a saucepan and cover with water. Bring to the boil and cook until just tender, about 8 minutes, then drain and let them steam dry.

Put 1 tablespoon of the vegetable oil into a roasting tin and heat in the oven for a few minutes. Take out of the oven, add the chips and turn to coat with the oil, then spread them out in a single layer. Return to the oven and roast for about 40 minutes until golden, turning a few times during roasting.

Meanwhile, make the curry sauce. Mix the curry powder, turmeric, pepper, cinnamon and ginger together in a small bowl and set aside. Heat the remaining oil in a saucepan over a medium heat and sauté the onion, garlic and apples for 5 minutes. The apples will start to break down a little. Add the curry powder mix and cook for 1 minute, stirring. Add the flour and give it a good mix. Now gradually add the stock and keep stirring all the time so there are no lumps. Stir in the vinegar, Worcestershire sauce, sugar and orange juice (if using).

Reduce down over a medium heat, stirring occasionally, until the sauce starts to thicken, about 10-15 minutes. Take off the heat, then blend to your desired consistency with a stick blender. Add the raisins (if using) and season to taste with salt - be careful because the stock will be quite salty. Keep warm.

When the chips are done, place on plates and pour a ton of the curry sauce over each portion.

SPICED SALT & PEPPER CHIPS

SERVES 4

These go down a right treat in our gaff alongside a stir-fry. Great Friday night take-away. Certainly cheaper.

1kg potatoes, skin on

3½ tbsp vegetable oil

1½ tsp Chinese five spice powder

1 tsp garlic powder

1 tsp onion powder

½ tsp salt

½ tsp pepper

1½ tsp caster sugar

¼ tsp chilli flakes

½ onion, cut into chunks

1 green pepper, deseeded and cut into chunks

1 red pepper, deseeded and cut into chunks

Preheat the oven to 180°C fan/200°C/gas mark 6.

Cut the potatoes into chips. Rinse under cold water, then place the potatoes in a saucepan and cover with water. Bring to the boil and cook until just tender, about 8 minutes. Drain and let them steam dry.

Now put 2 tablespoons of the vegetable oil in a roasting tin and heat in the oven for 5 minutes. Take out of the oven, then add the chips. Give them a good mix, spread the chips out in a single layer, then place back in the oven. After 20 minutes, take the tin out and stir the chips. Place back in the oven for another 20 minutes until the chips are nice and crispy.

While the chips are cooking, put the five spice powder, garlic and onion powder, salt, pepper, sugar and chilli flakes in a small bowl and mix well. Set aside.

When the chips are done, take them out of the oven and put to one side. Now add the remaining 1½ tablespoons of oil to a large frying pan or wok over a medium-high heat. Add the onion and peppers and stir-fry until nice and softened, about 5 minutes.

Now put the chips in with the onion and peppers. Stir well. Add the spiced salt and pepper mix and stir well for a minute or two over the heat. Serve up and enjoy.

CHIP COBS & LIQUID GOLD

SERVES 4

Roasting the leftover chicken carcass is the key for this. Gives it such flavour to build on. Building flavour is what's it all about. This is nectar in a cob. Don't be shy adding the liquid gold to ya cobs. Enjoy.

1 leftover chicken carcass, roughly chopped/broken into a few pieces

1 onion, quartered

1 small garlic bulb, cut in half horizontally

1 carrot, peeled and cut into chunks

drizzle of vegetable oil

2 tbsp plain flour

300ml dry cider

½ tbsp Worcestershire sauce

½ tsp caster sugar

¼ tsp salt

¼ tsp pepper

1 x quantity home-made plain chips (from the Chip Shop Curry Sauce and Chips recipe on page 150)

4 crusty cob rolls, split in half

Preheat the oven to 180°C fan/200°C/gas mark 6.

Place the chicken carcass in a roasting tin with the onion, garlic and carrot. Drizzle with a little vegetable oil, then roast in the oven for 30 minutes. This gives the gravy depth of flavour.

Remove from the oven and place the tin on the hob over a low heat. Add the flour and mix well, then stir in the cider, scraping up all the bits from the bottom of the tin. Bring to a simmer, stirring. Transfer the mixture to a large saucepan, then add 1 litre of water, bring to a simmer and simmer uncovered for 1 hour.

Strain the gravy into another saucepan, making sure you push all the flavour out of the chicken and vegetables (then discard these). Return to the heat and add the Worcestershire sauce, sugar, salt and pepper. Stir and simmer until nice, smooth and thickened, about 8–10 minutes.

To serve, I recommend you make plain chips (see the Chips part of the Chip Shop Curry Sauce and Chips recipe on page 150), simply seasoned with salt and pepper. Pile a load of chips into the cobs. You will have enough chips for the side as well. Now pour the gravy into 4 small bowls. Place on the plates alongside the chip cobs and chips. Dip your chip cob into the gravy and enjoy the fruits of your labour. This is a mind-blowing gravy!

 You can freeze this gravy for up to 3 months. Just defrost and reheat until hot before serving.

CRISPY 'SEAWEED'

SERVES 4

This is a nice side dish if you're making home-made Chinese. The crispy leaves are so addictive!

6-8 leaves of fresh greens
  (spring greens)
vegetable oil, for frying
1½ tsp caster sugar
good pinch of salt

Remove the stalks from the leaves of the greens. Don't throw away the stalks - you can use them in a stir-fry. Now stack the leaves on top of each other and roll them up like a cigar. Thinly slice, then spread them over your chopping board. Pat dry any moisture with kitchen paper.

Pour enough vegetable oil into a saucepan to come up to a depth of around 4cm. Place over a medium heat and heat until hot - you don't want it to be screaming hot because when you add the leaves it will spit a bit. Be careful. Test the oil by dropping a piece of leaf in and if it floats to the top and starts to bubble, the oil is ready.

Now carefully add the half of the leaves to the hot oil and fry, stirring from time to time. Don't be afraid to turn the heat up or down as needed, and keep your eye on them all the time. When the leaves start to colour to a light brown stage and are crispy (this will take about 8 minutes), take them out using a slotted spoon or spider strainer and drain on kitchen paper. Repeat with the remaining leaves.

Place the crispy leaves in a serving bowl, sprinkle over the sugar and salt and mix well. Serve straight away.

 You could use Savoy cabbage, if you can't get fresh greens.

THE F.T.T. – FRENCH TOAST TOASTIE

SERVES 2 (MAKES 2 SANDWICHES)

This idea came to me one Christmas many moons ago. It makes a great Boxing Day breakfast.

100ml milk

2 eggs

1 tsp caster sugar

1 tsp vanilla extract

½ tsp ground cinnamon

¼ tsp ground nutmeg

knob of butter, plus extra for spreading

4 thick slices of white sliced bread

2 tbsp cranberry sauce

½ red onion, sliced

160g Brie, sliced

splash of vegetable oil

salt and pepper

In a bowl, mix together the milk, eggs, sugar, vanilla, cinnamon, nutmeg and a pinch each of salt and pepper. Put to one side.

Now butter the slices of bread on one side, then spread the cranberry sauce over 2 slices. Top with the onion and Brie slices and season with salt and pepper. Now place the other 2 bread slices on top, buttered-side down, to make 2 sandwiches, and press down hard.

Add the knob of butter and a splash of vegetable oil to a large frying pan over a medium heat (or use a smaller frying pan and cook each sandwich separately). When the butter starts to foam, grab the sandwiches, one at a time, and place in the egg mixture. Flip to cover both sides completely and then place in the pan, side-by-side (or cook each sandwich separately).

When the sandwiches start to go golden on the bottom, flip them over. When they're nice and golden and crispy on both sides, transfer them to serving plates, cut in half and enjoy.

THE VAMPIRE SLAYER

SERVES 4–6

I made this garlic bread when I appeared on *The Great Cookbook Challenge*. It had a mixed response to how much garlic was in it. Basically, in my words, I said if ya gonna have garlic bread, ya gonna have a ton of garlic in it. 'Nuff said.

1 baguette

1 garlic bulb

2 tsp vegetable oil

3 spring onions, chopped

2 tbsp chopped parsley

250g butter, softened

zest of 1 lemon

¼ tsp salt

¼ tsp pepper

Preheat the oven to 180°C fan/200°C/gas mark 6.

Cut the baguette in half widthways (across the middle), then cut both halves into slices at 3cm intervals, but don't cut all the way through. Put to one side and cover with a tea towel.

Cut the garlic bulb in half horizontally. Rub the vegetable oil over the cut sides and wrap in foil. Roast in the oven for around 30-40 minutes until tender.

Take out of the oven and squeeze the garlic flesh into a bowl. Add the rest of the ingredients and mix well. Now spread this mixture into the cuts on the 2 baguette halves. Put plenty in and also rub some of the mixture all over the baguette. Wrap the baguette halves in foil and bake in the oven for around 30 minutes.

Take out of the oven and loosen the foil to expose the baguettes. Put back in the oven for another 5-10 minutes to crisp up. Take out and enjoy.

CAULIFLOWER CHEESE

SERVES 4-6

Another must at the Sunday roast table. Crispy and gooey. All the good stuff.
Warning: make sure you make enough to go around. You'll need it!

1 cauliflower, around 700g

1½ tbsp butter

1½ tbsp plain flour

250ml milk

100g mature Cheddar
cheese, grated

½ tsp English mustard

¼ tsp ground nutmeg

good pinch of cayenne
pepper

salt and pepper

Preheat the oven to 180°C fan/200°C/gas mark 6.

Remove the central stalk from the cauliflower, then pull apart
the cauliflower florets. Place in a saucepan and cover with
water. Bring to a rolling boil, then cook until just tender, about
5-8 minutes. Drain and leave to steam dry.

Meanwhile, melt the butter in a separate saucepan over a
medium-low heat. Stir in the flour, then let it cook out for a few
minutes, stirring all the time. Now start adding the milk, bit by bit.
Keep stirring until all the milk has been added. Reduce the heat
to low and continue to cook, stirring. When it starts to thicken,
add half the cheese. Turn off the heat, then stir in the mustard,
nutmeg and a good pinch each of salt and pepper.

Now put your cauliflower into an ovenproof dish (approx.
23 x 18 x 5cm). Spoon over the sauce, then sprinkle the rest of
the cheese all over. Sprinkle with the cayenne pepper. Bake in
the oven for around 30 minutes. It is done when the cheese is
golden and bubbling. Enjoy.

MANGO SALSA

SERVES 4

So fresh and vibrant. Goes so well with barbecued or grilled chicken and pork, especially my Jerk Chicken on page 172.

1 ripe mango
½ red pepper, deseeded
½ yellow pepper, deseeded
4 spring onions, sliced
½ small red chilli, chopped
½ small green chilli, chopped
juice of ½ lemon
juice of ½ lime
2 tsp olive oil
½ tsp honey
salt and pepper

Peel the mango. There's a stone in it so cut either side of the stone - you will have 2 sections of flesh. Chop this into small chunks, then cut around the stone for more flesh and chop into small chunks. Place in a bowl.

Next, place the pepper halves (one at a time), skin-side down, over a gas ring and leave until charred (if you don't have a gas hob, see Tip). Be careful and use tongs to turn then remove the pepper. Once they are both charred, place in a bowl and cover with clingfilm (this will loosen the skin). Set aside for 5 minutes.

Put the spring onions and chillies into the bowl with the mango. Now take the clingfilm off the peppers, then with the back of a knife, scrape off most of the skin, leaving a bit of char on - it's flavour. Chop up the peppers and add to the mango bowl. Now add the lemon and lime juices, the olive oil, honey and a good pinch each of salt and pepper, and give it a good mix. Leave in the fridge for 2-3 hours to let the flavours develop, and bring back to room temperature before serving.

To char peppers without a gas hob, simply place the pepper halves, skin-side up, on a rack under a preheated hot grill and grill until charred.

SAUSAGE MEAT & CIDER STUFFING

SERVES 4-6

This is a banger ('scuse the pun!). I woke up in the middle of the night and thought of this and had to write it down.

100g dried stuffing mix (I use sage and onion)

1 eating apple, peeled, cored and chopped into small chunks

3 Cumberland sausages

1 tsp English mustard

200ml dry cider

½ onion, chopped

½ tsp caster sugar

salt and pepper

Preheat the oven to 180°C fan/200°C/gas mark 6.

Put the stuffing mix into a bowl and add the apple chunks. Take the skin off the sausages and add the sausage meat to the bowl. Add the mustard and a good pinch each of salt and pepper and mix.

Put the cider and onion into a saucepan, bring to the boil over a medium heat, then turn the heat off. Stir the sugar into the cider, then pour the cider all over the stuffing mixture and give it a good mix.

Spoon into an ovenproof dish (approx. 18 x 15 x 6cm), then bake in the oven for around 30 minutes. It will be done when the top is nice and crisp, but it will still be a bit fluffy on the inside. Serve.

IAN'S LEGENDARY EASY PICKLED EGGS

MAKES 15

I've been doing these every Christmas for 20 years or so. I start to pickle the eggs around the end of October so they will be ready for Christmastime. They go so well with cold cuts and pickles. I also like to give some away as presents. People love them. A great recipe to start off your pickling game.

200ml distilled white vinegar

1 tbsp caster sugar

1 tsp salt

½ onion, chopped into big chunks

1 red chilli, seeds in, cut into chunks

1 green chilli, seeds in, cut into chunks

1 tsp mustard seeds

1 bay leaf

1 tsp black peppercorns

15 medium eggs

You'll need a 1.2 litre jar with a lid.

Add the vinegar, 200ml of water and the sugar to a saucepan. Bring to the boil to dissolve the sugar, then add the salt and give it a stir. Take the pan off the heat and stir in the onion, chillies, mustard seeds, bay leaf and peppercorns. Give it a stir and put to one side to cool.

Preheat the oven to 140°C fan/160°C/gas mark 3.

Wash your jar and lid well, then rinse and place both into a pan of boiling water and boil for 5 minutes. Take out, drain and place the jar and lid onto a baking tray, then place in the oven for 5 minutes to sterilise them. Remove from the oven and leave to cool.

Now place the eggs in a large saucepan and cover with water. Place over a medium-high heat and bring to the boil. Turn down to a rolling boil and set a timer for 8 minutes. When the time is up, drain and crack the eggs, then place under cold running water for 5 minutes. After 5 minutes, peel the eggs under cold water, making sure there is no shell left on them.

Once peeled, place a few eggs in the sterilised jar, pour in some pickling mixture, then repeat until you have filled up the jar. Make sure you put all the spices and bay leaf in. Now put the lid on. Give it a turn. Place in a cool cupboard and turn from time to time.

The pickled eggs are ready in a week, but they're even better the longer you leave them. They'll keep in a dark cupboard for 4 months if unopened. Once opened, keep in the fridge and eat within 2 weeks.

- ~~JERK CHICKEN LEGS~~ & WITH MANGO (WOULD WORK WITH VEGTABLES AS WELL)
- CHARLED VEG MEDITARANION STYLE
- PERI PERI CHICKEN ✓
- KOFTAS BURGERS
- ~~BURGERS~~
- PIMPED UP CORN ON THE COB ✓
- CHERRY TOMATOES & HALLOUMI SKEWRS WITH A GARLIC & LEMON DRESSING
  - BACK YARD BEANS
- TANDORI CHICKEN ✓
- MACKREII
- ~~STICKY CHICKEN~~ THIGHS
  - JERK CHICKEN COCONUT RICE MAGO SALSA ✓
  - GRAPE FRUIT GRILLED CHICKEN

CHEESE BURGERS WITH THE CHEESE BURGER SAUCE

LEMON & LIME WINGS ✓

CHAR SIU ~~PIGS~~ PIGS IN BLANKETS

BOMBAY PIGS IN BLANKETS

CHAR SIU CHICKEN THIGHS. ✓

CHICKEN BURGER WITH ULTIMATE CHEESE BURGER SAUCE

TASTY CORN ON THE COB

SERVES 4

If ya love ya corn, you'll love this. I can't get enough of this juicy corn with a cold lager on a hot summer's day, chatting with family and friends.

3 tbsp mayonnaise

1 spring onion, finely chopped

1 tsp hot sauce (of your choice)

½ tsp garlic powder

1 tsp chopped coriander

zest of 1 lime

juice of ½ lime

4 x 250g corn on the cobs, husks and silk removed

70g mature Cheddar cheese

salt and pepper

Preheat the barbecue.

In a bowl, mix all the ingredients together, except the corn cobs and cheese, and season with a good pinch each of salt and pepper.

Place the corn cobs on the grill rack directly over the hot coals on the barbecue. Keep turning as the corn cooks to build up some char - you will hear the corn popping and that's when you turn. Once you have a good colour all over, after about 8-10 minutes, remove and place on a serving plate.

Brush the mayonnaise mixture all over the corn cobs. Put plenty on. Grate the cheese over, giving the corn cobs a good coating. The mayonnaise mixture enables the cheese to stick. Tuck in and enjoy.

 The mayo mixture also makes a great dip.

TANDOORI BARBECUED CHICKEN

SERVES 4

This is my take on tandoori chicken. It falls off the bone if it's done right and you can taste all the spices topped with the smokiness and charring from the barbecue. You'll be going back for more, that's for sure.

3 garlic cloves, crushed

5cm piece of fresh ginger, peeled and minced

zest and juice of 1 lemon

6 heaped tbsp natural yogurt

1 tbsp honey

½ tbsp vegetable oil

1 tbsp tandoori curry powder or medium curry powder

1 tsp paprika

1 tsp ground cumin

1 tsp ground coriander

½ tsp chilli powder

¼ tsp ground cinnamon

¼ tsp salt

¼ tsp pepper

couple of drops of red food colouring (optional)

1kg chicken thighs, bone-in and skin-on

Mix together all the ingredients, except the chicken, in a large bowl.

Take the skin off the chicken thighs (this is optional) and then make 3 cuts down to the bone in each thigh. Don't throw away the skin - you can freeze it for later use.

Add the chicken thighs to the bowl of sauce, then rub the sauce all over the chicken and into the cuts. Cover with clingfilm and refrigerate for a minimum of 2 hours (but best overnight, if possible).

Preheat the barbecue.

When you are ready to barbecue, move the hot coals to one side so that you have direct heat and indirect heat areas. Place the chicken on the grill rack over the indirect heat, put the lid on and cook for around 15 minutes. Take the lid off and start to move the chicken over the direct heat, then just keep moving it from direct to indirect heat to build up some colour. Put the chicken back over the indirect heat and put the lid back on. Repeat this process until the internal temperature of the thickest part of the chicken thighs reaches 74°C/165°F and the juices run clear, about 40 minutes in total.

Enjoy the chicken thighs with side dishes such as Mediterranean Peppers (see page 186), Bombay Roast Potatoes (see page 144) and salad.

 You can use an oven to cook the chicken if you don't have a barbecue. Preheat the oven to 180°C fan/200°C/gas mark 6. Place the marinated chicken thighs in a shallow roasting tin (or on a baking tray) in a single layer. Roast in the oven for 40-45 minutes, turning once or twice, until cooked through (see above).

LEMON & LIME CHICKEN WINGS

SERVES 4

This is one of my faves. I've got great memories of eating these with me mate Ken who sadly passed away in the summer of 2021. I would cook up a load of these, and whether it was a baking hot day in the summer or a freezing winter's night, we would do it. In Ken's own words, these are a game changer. And Ken, you were definitely right - something so simple but so zingy and nice. Do the simple things right and you're halfway there.

1kg chicken wings
½ tsp salt
½ tsp pepper
zest and juice of 2 lemons
zest and juice of 2 limes
2 garlic cloves, crushed
2 tsp honey
½ tsp vegetable oil

Preheat the barbecue.

Place the wings in a bowl. Season with ¼ teaspoon each of the salt and pepper. Put to one side.

Now mix all the other ingredients together in a separate bowl, including the remaining salt and pepper, to make a dressing for basting.

Set the barbecue up with the hot coals on one side so you have direct heat and indirect heat areas. Place the wings on the grill rack over the indirect heat and put the lid on. Cook for 10 minutes. Take the lid off and move the wings over the direct heat and keep turning. When you start to get some colour on the wings, move them back over the indirect heat. Baste the wings with some of the dressing, then put the lid back on. Repeat this basting process several times over a period of 20-30 minutes. The wings are done when they are nice and golden with some charring in places.

 If the lemons and limes are small, use 3 of each.

JERK CHICKEN & COCONUT RICE WITH MANGO SALSA

SERVES 4

Don't be put off making this jerk chicken by the long list of ingredients. It's mainly storecupboard ingredients so they won't go off in a hurry. Plus it stocks up your storecupboard. This jerk is more on the fruity side in flavour, not blow your socks off, but boy does it deliver on flavour - and such a depth of flavour. I can assure you, you'll be making this forever more. Please give it a go - you won't be disappointed.

For the jerk chicken

1 onion, quartered

4 spring onions, roughly chopped

1 red chilli, chopped

1 green chilli, chopped

5 garlic cloves, peeled

thumb-sized piece of fresh ginger, peeled and sliced

2 tsp ground allspice

½ tsp ground cinnamon

½ tsp ground nutmeg

½ tsp ground cumin

½ tsp chilli flakes

1 tsp dried thyme

zest and juice of 2 limes

zest and juice of 1 lemon

3 tbsp soy sauce

3 tbsp Worcestershire sauce

3 tbsp malt vinegar

1 tbsp vegetable oil

1 tbsp soft dark brown sugar

¼ tsp salt

¼ tsp pepper

4 chicken legs, skin on

For the coconut rice

1 tbsp unsalted butter

1 garlic clove, chopped

5cm piece of fresh ginger, peeled and chopped

200g jasmine rice

200ml coconut milk

zest of 1 lime

2 tsp caster sugar

salt and pepper

To serve

Mango Salsa (see page 160)

Put all the ingredients for the jerk chicken, minus the chicken legs, into a food processor and blitz until well combined into a paste. Put to one side.

Take your chicken legs and score each 2 or 3 times down to the bone. Place them in a large bowl or on a food tray. Pour three-quarters of the jerk mixture over the chicken and rub it really well into the cuts and all over the chicken. Save the rest of the marinade to baste the chicken when cooking (put it into a covered bowl and refrigerate). Cover the chicken and place in the fridge to marinate for a minimum of 3 hours (but best overnight, if possible).

Preheat the barbecue.

When it's time to cook, move the hot coals to one side of the barbecue so you have direct heat and indirect heat areas. Place the chicken legs on the grill rack over the indirect heat and place the lid on. Cook for 10-15 minutes. Take the lid off and start to introduce the chicken legs to the direct heat. Keep flipping the chicken. When you start to get some colour, move the chicken back over the indirect heat.

This is the time to start basting the chicken, so baste the legs with some of the reserved marinade. Put the lid back on and cook for another 10 minutes. Repeat the process of direct heat and basting, then put the lid back on and cook for another 10 minutes. Do this a couple of times more to give a total cooking time of 40 minutes. The chicken legs are done when they're nice and golden with some charring in places and the internal temperature of the thickest part of the chicken legs reaches 74°C/165°F and the juices run clear. Keep warm in a low oven until you are ready to serve.

While the chicken is cooking, make the coconut rice. Melt the butter in a saucepan over a medium heat, then add the garlic and ginger and cook for 2 minutes. Rinse and drain your rice, then add to the pan, stirring. Cook for 1 minute. Stir in the coconut milk, 200ml of water, the lime zest, sugar and a good pinch each of salt and pepper. Bring to the boil, then give it a stir, cover, reduce the heat and simmer for 12 minutes. Don't be tempted to stir. When the time is up, take it off the heat and fluff up the rice with a fork. Put the lid back on and let it stand for 5 minutes. Serve the barbecued chicken legs with the coconut rice and mango salsa. Enjoy.

You can use an oven to cook the chicken if you don't have a barbecue. Preheat the oven to 180°C fan/200°C/gas mark 6. Place the marinated chicken legs in a shallow roasting tin (or on a baking tray) in a single layer. Roast in the oven for 45-50 minutes, turning once or twice and basting, until cooked through (see above).

JUICY JUMBO PRAWNS

SERVES 4-5

This is a great appetiser to get the taste buds buzzing. You'll think you're in the Mediterranean with this one. Winner all round.

350g raw peeled jumbo prawns

½ tbsp vegetable oil

2 tsp harissa paste

3 garlic cloves, crushed

1 tbsp chopped parsley

zest of ½ lemon and juice of 1 lemon

zest of ½ lime and juice of 1 lime

½ tsp caster sugar

¼ tsp salt

¼ tsp pepper

You will need 4-5 metal or wooden skewers.

If you are using frozen prawns, defrost them, then check to see if they have been deveined. If not, get a sharp knife. On the back of each prawn you will see a black vein running along it. Cut along that, pull the vein out and discard. Once you have done that, mix all the remaining ingredients together in a bowl. Add the prawns and coat them well, then cover and leave to marinate for 1 hour in the fridge.

While the prawns are marinating, if you are using wooden skewers, soak them in water. This will stop them burning.

Now preheat the barbecue. When the coals are glowing, that's when it's ready to cook.

Take your prawns and push a skewer through the middle of each one, putting 3 or 4 prawns on each skewer, depending on how many servings you want (I like three on mine). Keep the marinade.

Now put the prawn skewers on the grill rack directly over the hot coals and spoon some of the marinade over. Cook for 3-4 minutes, then turn and spoon over more marinade. Cook for another 3-4 minutes. Then they're done (they will have turned pink), so tuck in.

You can use a griddle pan if you don't have a barbecue. Preheat a griddle pan over a high heat until hot, then add the prawn skewers and griddle them, basting and turning as above, until cooked, about 6-8 minutes.

CHINESE BARBECUED CHICKEN CHAR SIU

SERVES 4-6 WITH SIDES

This one will have you licking ya fingers without a doubt. One of my all-time favourites to do on the barbecue. You want to build up a really good char on the chicken. Really caramelise it. It's not burnt - it's flavour. Adding the food colouring really enhances it, and visually it just makes you want to eat it!

2 tbsp hoisin sauce

1 tbsp soy sauce

1 tbsp tomato ketchup

1 tbsp honey

1 tbsp soft brown sugar (light or dark)

½ tbsp malt vinegar

juice of ½ orange

2 tsp Chinese five spice powder

1 tsp Worcestershire sauce

½ tsp sesame oil

2 garlic cloves, crushed

thumb-sized piece of fresh ginger, peeled and minced

½ tsp salt

½ tsp pepper

5 drops of red food colouring (optional)

6 medium-large chicken thighs, bone-in, skin-on

Mix together all the ingredients, except the chicken, in a bowl and set aside.

Now score each chicken thigh twice down to the bone. Place the chicken thighs into a container, pour half the marinade mix over the chicken and give it a good rub all over the thighs and into the cuts. Cover and leave to marinate in the fridge overnight. Reserve the rest of the marinade to baste the chicken when cooking (put it into a covered bowl and refrigerate).

On the day of the cook, preheat the barbecue.

Set your barbecue up with the hot coals on one side so you have direct heat and indirect heat areas. Place the chicken thighs on the grill rack over the indirect heat. Put the lid on and cook for 10 minutes. Take the lid off and move the chicken thighs over the direct heat and keep turning for a few minutes. When you see colour on them, move the chicken thighs back over the indirect heat and start basting the chicken with the reserved marinade. Put the lid back on. Repeat the basting process every 7 minutes or so to build up a nice and sticky glaze. Cook the chicken for around 30-40 minutes in total. It will be ready when it's nice and sticky, almost burnt in places, and the internal temperature reaches 74°C/165°F when a thermometer is placed into the thickest part of the thighs and the juices run clear.

I like to eat these with Vampire Slayer garlic bread (see page 157) and Nutty Noodle Salad (see page 80).

PERI PERI CHICKEN

SERVES 4-6

Classic flavours. So easy to do. So good on the barbecue. This is one you'll be doing week in week out during the summer months or even all year round if you're like me (a barbecue is for life, not just the summer).

1 onion, roughly chopped

5 garlic cloves, roughly chopped

½ red pepper, deseeded and chopped

½ yellow pepper, deseeded and chopped

½ red chilli

zest and juice of 1 large lemon

3 tbsp cider vinegar

3 tbsp vegetable oil

½ tbsp chopped thyme or ½ tsp dried thyme

1 tsp smoked paprika

1 tsp paprika

½ tsp chilli flakes

½ tsp caster sugar

¼ tsp salt

¼ tsp pepper

1kg chicken thighs, bone-in, skin-on

Put all the ingredients, except the chicken, into a saucepan. Bring to the boil over a medium heat, then simmer for 5 minutes. Take off the heat and leave it to cool.

Make 2 incisions down to the bone in each chicken thigh. Place the thighs in a large bowl.

When the peri peri mixture is cool, transfer it to a food processor and blitz until smooth. Pour a generous half of the peri peri sauce all over the chicken and toss to coat all the chicken thighs well. Reserve the rest of the peri peri sauce to baste the chicken during cooking (put it into a covered bowl and refrigerate). Cover and refrigerate the chicken for a minimum of 3 hours (or ideally overnight).

Preheat the barbecue.

When you are ready to cook, move the hot coals to one side of the barbecue to create indirect heat and direct heat areas. Place the marinated chicken thighs on the grill rack over the indirect heat and put the lid on. Cook for 10 minutes, then move the chicken over the direct heat and keep turning. When the chicken is starting to show colour, move it back over the indirect heat. Start to baste the chicken with the reserved peri peri marinade. Put the lid back on and cook for another 10 minutes, then repeat 2 or 3 more times. This should take around 30 minutes in total. The chicken is done when the internal temperature of the thickest part of the chicken thighs reaches 74°C/165°F and the juices run clear.

You can use an oven to cook the chicken if you don't have a barbecue. Preheat the oven to 180°C fan/200°C/gas mark 6. Place the marinated chicken thighs in a shallow roasting tin (or on a baking tray) in a single layer. Roast in the oven for 40-45 minutes, turning once or twice and basting, until cooked through (see above).

BURSE'S BONFIRE BANGERS

SERVES 4

Burse is my nickname so the name of this rolls off the tongue. This is inspired by a recipe my brother Mark makes. It is such low maintenance to do on the barbecue. You just leave it alone and check from time to time. So you can enjoy the fireworks, plus it's very filling. Great stuff.

12 Cumberland sausages

1 onion, chopped

3 garlic cloves, chopped

½ red chilli, chopped

½ green chilli, chopped

300ml vegetable stock

300ml dry cider

4 tbsp apple sauce

2 tbsp cider vinegar

1 tbsp Dijon mustard

1 tbsp caster sugar

¼ tsp salt

¼ tsp pepper

1 x 400g can butter beans, drained and rinsed

4 x 15cm baguettes

Preheat the barbecue.

Place your sausages in a foil tray (approx. 30 x 20 x 4cm).

Now in a jug, mix all the remaining ingredients together, except the butter beans and baguettes. Take the sausages and sauce out to the barbecue.

Take the sausages out of the foil tray, place them on the grill rack over the barbecue and brown them on all sides for a few minutes. Now put the sausages back into the foil tray, place the tray on the grill rack directly over the hot coals and pour the sauce all over them. Bring to a simmer, then put the lid on. Keep checking from time to time. You may have to top up the sauce with a little water and turn the tray occasionally. The sausages are cooked when they are tender and the onion is soft – this will take around 1 hour in total, depending on how hot your barbecue is. The sauce should be reduced and a bit sticky by this stage.

After about 40 minutes, tip the beans into the foil tray with the sausages.

To serve, slice open the baguettes and place 3 sausages in each one, then top with loads of the sauce. Enjoy.

KOFTA BURGERS WITH MINTED YOGURT

SERVES 5

This is a banging burger and a great twist on your typical lamb Kofta. I use beef because it's much cheaper (lamb is out the window) and is a lot easier to get your hands on. I like the fact that it's beef but it still packs a punch and doesn't take away from the classic Kofta taste.

For the burgers

1kg minced beef
  (15-20 per cent fat)
1 onion, chopped
4 garlic cloves, crushed
½ tsp pepper
3 tsp chopped red chilli
3 tsp chopped green chilli
4 tbsp chopped parsley
4 tsp dried oregano
4 tsp ground cumin
4 tsp ground coriander
2 tsp paprika
½ tsp cayenne pepper
½ tsp caster sugar
½ tsp salt

For the minted yogurt

250g Greek yogurt
½ red onion, finely diced
2 garlic cloves, minced
zest and juice of ½ lemon
3 tsp mint sauce
½ tsp caster sugar
salt and pepper

To serve

5 burger buns, cut in half
shredded lettuce
tomato slices
sliced red onion

Put all the burger ingredients into a bowl and mix and squeeze together with your hands. Cover and refrigerate for 30 minutes.

Divide the burger mix into 5 equal portions and shape into burgers. Place on a tray and freeze for 30 minutes before cooking (this firms them up so they don't fall apart on the barbecue).

Meanwhile, preheat the barbecue.

Mix all the minted yogurt ingredients together in a bowl along with a good pinch each of salt and pepper, then set aside.

Now move your hot coals to one side of the barbecue so you have direct heat and indirect heat areas. Once the coals are ready, take your burgers to the barbecue. Place them on the grill rack over the direct heat. Don't be tempted to move them. Flip them over when you can slide a fish spatula under and they don't stick. Cook until coloured, then move the burgers over the indirect heat. Place the lid on and cook for 10-15 minutes. Now take the lid off and move them over the direct heat for more flavour and char. They are done when they are still juicy but the juice is clear.

To serve, toast the burger buns, then spread some minted yogurt onto the bottom halves. Add some lettuce, tomato and red onion to each. Place the burgers on top, followed by more minted yogurt, then top with the bun lids. Tuck in!

THE THIGH IS THE LIMIT – APPLE-SMOKED TURKEY THIGH

SERVES 4–6 HUNGRY PEOPLE

You must try this. Such a taste sensation with all the flavour coming through from the rub and the sweet smoky flavour from the apple wood. Bang on.

1½ tbsp onion powder

1½ tbsp garlic powder

2 tbsp caster sugar

1½ tbsp paprika

2 tsp salt

1 tsp pepper

1 tsp dried rosemary

1 tsp dried thyme

½ tsp cayenne pepper

1 tbsp American classic yellow mustard (I like French's)

1 turkey thigh joint, around 1.25kg, bone-in and skin-on

To serve

4–6 crusty cob rolls or other rolls of your choice

Pear and Apple Slaw (see page 142)

Preheat the barbecue. You'll also need some apple wood chunks for the barbecue.

Mix together all the ingredients, except the mustard and turkey, in a bowl to make the rub.

Now take your turkey thigh and push an upturned spoon under the skin to create a pocket. Rub the mustard all over the turkey and under the skin. Make sure it's all covered – this helps the rub stick to the turkey and adds flavour. Now sprinkle the turkey all over with the rub, including under the skin, and pat it in place. Don't rub the spice rub on, just pat it (if you rub, the spices will clump up). Use all the rub. It may seem a lot, but trust me it works.

Now move your hot coals to one side of the barbecue so you have direct heat and indirect heat areas. Once the coals are ready, place a chunk of apple wood just to the side of the coals so it starts to smoulder. Now place the turkey on the grill rack over the indirect heat and pop the lid on. The turkey should take around 1 hour 20 minutes–2 hours to cook, depending on how hot your coals are. Turn the turkey a couple of times during cooking. It's done when you put a meat thermometer into the thickest part of the thigh and it reads 79°C/175°F and the juices run clear. Remove the turkey from the barbecue, cover in foil and leave to rest for 30 minutes, then carve to serve.

Pile the hot turkey into split cob rolls or other rolls. Dollop loads of pear and apple slaw on top and enjoy.

MEDITERRANEAN PEPPERS

SERVES 2-4

These are a must at any barbecue. Simple but effective. A great little number as a side dish, especially with barbecued meats. Yum.

1 large red pepper, deseeded and cut into thick slices

1 large yellow pepper, deseeded and cut into thick slices

1 red onion, cut into large chunks

3 garlic cloves, crushed

zest of ½ lime and juice of 1 lime

zest of ½ lemon and juice of 1 lemon

1 tbsp tomato purée

1 tsp honey

1 tsp dried basil

1 tsp dried oregano

1 tsp smoked paprika

½ tsp chilli flakes

¼ tsp salt

¼ tsp pepper

Mix all the ingredients together in a large bowl, then cover and leave to marinate at room temperature for 1 hour.

Preheat the barbecue.

When the coals are glowing, it's time to cook. I've got a barbecue fish grilling grate/basket which I like to use (if you haven't got one you can thread the peppers and onion onto metal skewers - if you use wooden skewers, soak them in water for 1 hour before use to stop them burning).

Take your peppers and onion out of the marinade, place them in the fish grate/basket in a single layer and close the grate/basket. Keep the marinade. Now place the grate/basket on the grill rack directly over the hot coals and spoon the marinade over. Keep turning the veg every minute or two and keep basting them with the marinade. The peppers and onion are done when they are nice and charred on both sides (this will take about 10 minutes in total). Serve hot.

APPLE & HALLOUMI SKEWERS

SERVES 2-4

The saltiness from the halloumi goes so well with the sweetness from the apples and honey. Great contrast in flavours.

½ tsp black peppercorns

½ tsp flaky sea salt

½ tsp fennel seeds

½ tsp dried rosemary

1 tbsp honey

1 tbsp vegetable oil

2 tsp cider vinegar

good pinch of ground cinnamon

1 x 225g pack halloumi cheese

3 small eating apples

You will need 6 metal or wooden skewers. If you are using wooden skewers, soak them in water for 1 hour – this will stop them burning.

Preheat the barbecue.

To make the dressing, put the peppercorns, salt, fennel seeds and rosemary in a pestle and mortar and grind to a powder, then transfer to a bowl. Add the honey, vegetable oil, vinegar and cinnamon and mix well, then put to one side.

Now cut your halloumi into 12 blocks. Quarter and core your apples (leave the skin on). Start by putting a piece of apple onto each skewer, followed by a piece of halloumi, then apple, then halloumi – so you have 2 pieces of apple and 2 pieces of halloumi on each skewer.

Place the skewers on the grill rack directly over the hot coals and brush some of the dressing over the halloumi and apples. Turn from time to time and keep basting. They are done when the apples are slightly caramelised and the halloumi is charred – this will take about 8 minutes in total. Tuck in!

tip

Soak the halloumi in cold water in the fridge overnight, then drain before using. This stops it breaking when putting it on the skewers.

- GRANNY D'S EGG CUSTARD
- JAMMY DODGER BANOFFEE PIE ?
- APPLE & FRUIT PIE
- CARREMEISED BANNAN PANCKES/CREPES
- CHOCOLATE BARK SOME KIND
- ROCKY ROAD
- FRUIT SALAD / WITH CHILLI FLAKES
- BANANA SPLIT / WITH SOME KIND OF SPICES
          (CRISPY ONIONS)

- CORN FLAKE TART/CAKE
- BLACKBERRY & APPLE CRUMBLE WITH GINGER BISUITS
- SWEET TOASTIE
- YORKSHIRE PUDDIN) WITH GARLIC /ONION
  CHUTNEY & PAN GRAVY

- YORKSHIRE PUDDIN) IN THE BATTER
  CINNAMON / NUT MEG /CHILLI FLAKES / HONEY.
  COOK AND TOP ALL WITH A ATUM FRUIT
  COMPOT DUST WITH ICING SUGAR. (?)
- PEAR /APPLE /BALCAMIC CRUMBLE ✓
- BREAD & BUTTER PUDDING
- BLACKBERRY FOL WITH GINGER BISCITS TOP ✓
- LEFT OVER DOGHNUTS BREAD PUDDING ✓

- TOFFEE APPLES

PUDDING

PEAR, APPLE & BALSAMIC CRUMBLE

SERVES 4-6

We do love a good crumble. We have a cooking apple tree in our garden and the neighbour has a pear tree. So for us this crumble is cheap to make. Just ask around your friends and family, you'll be surprised how many people have fruit trees.

550g ripe pears

250g cooking apples

80g unsalted butter

50g caster sugar, plus 2 tbsp

1½ tsp balsamic vinegar

¼ tsp ground cinnamon

¼ tsp ground nutmeg

¼ tsp chilli flakes

100g plain flour

salt and pepper

Preheat the oven to 180°C fan/200°C/gas mark 6.

Peel and core the pears and apples, then chop into chunks. Melt 30g of the butter in a saucepan over a low-medium heat. Add the pear and apple chunks and give it a stir. Cook for a few minutes until the fruit starts to break down. Now add the 2 tablespoons of sugar and 100ml of water, along with the balsamic vinegar, cinnamon, nutmeg, chilli flakes and a good pinch each of salt and pepper. Let the mixture cook down and keep stirring. It's ready when it has reduced but still retains a bit of moisture, about 8-10 minutes. Put to one side.

In a bowl, add the flour and the remaining 50g of butter and the 50g of sugar and mix with your fingers to make a coarse crumb.

Put the fruit mix into an ovenproof dish (approx. 23 x 18 x 5cm), then spoon the crumble mixture evenly all over.

Bake in the oven for around 30 minutes. It's done when the crumble topping is nice and golden and bubbling. Serve with custard or ice cream.

BLACKBERRY FOOL & GINGER NUT TOPPING

SERVES 4

The cream cheese gives this such a silky smooth feeling. Topped with ginger nut biscuits to add texture. Spot on.

150g cream cheese

250ml double cream

3 tbsp icing sugar

1 tsp vanilla extract

100g Greek yogurt

200g fresh blackberries

2 tsp caster sugar

4 crunchy ginger biscuits
(I use Ginger Nuts)

Take the cream cheese out of the fridge 30 minutes in advance to let it soften.

Add the double cream to a large bowl with the icing sugar and vanilla. Whip together until the cream starts to stiffen (soft peak stage), but don't over-whip it. Now add the cream cheese and whisk until combined, then add the yogurt and fold it through. Set aside.

Place the blackberries in a separate bowl, putting a few aside to decorate. Sprinkle the caster sugar over the blackberries, then mush them up a bit with a fork, leaving some chunky.

Now spoon some of the mushed berries into the bottom of 4 clear glass ramekins or glasses, then spoon some cream mixture on top. Repeat 3 or so times, ending with a layer of the cream mixture.

Take your biscuits, put them into a food bag and smash into crumbs with a rolling pin, but leave them quite chunky. Decorate the desserts with the reserved blackberries, then sprinkle each dessert with the biscuit crumbs and serve.

You could make these ahead and chill in the fridge, then add the biscuit crumbs just before serving.

LEFTOVER DOUGHNUT BREAD PUDDING

SERVES 4

I came up with this tasty recipe having taken some doughnuts to share at my brother and his wife's home, but they didn't all get eaten, so they insisted I took them home with me. A couple of days later they had gone slightly stale and I didn't want to throw them away, so I made this - they were perfect for this easy pudding.

knob of butter

220g jam doughnuts (about 3 medium doughnuts)

220g custard doughnuts (about 3 medium doughnuts)

3 medium eggs

200ml milk

30g caster sugar

¼ tsp vanilla extract

¼ tsp ground nutmeg

¼ tsp ground cinnamon

Preheat the oven to 180°C fan/200°C/gas mark 6.

Grease a 20 x 20 x 5cm baking dish with the butter. Cut all the doughnuts into bite-sized pieces and place in the baking dish. Now crack your eggs into a bowl, add the rest of the ingredients and mix well. Pour the egg mixture over the doughnuts and press them down, then leave to soak for 10 minutes.

Bake in the oven for 30 minutes. I like mine crispy on top and gooey in the middle. If you want the middle to be more cooked, bake for a further 5-10 minutes. When the pudding is done, take it out of the oven and let it stand for 10 minutes before serving. Serve with ice cream or custard.

 Make sure the doughnuts are on the stale side so they soak up the egg mixture.

GOOEY GRENADES - YORKIES

SERVES 3-4 (MAKES 9)

I developed these from memories. When I was young my mum used to give me a slice of Yorkie with jam on before my dinner. So good. You could take these to a party and put them in the middle of the table for everyone to enjoy.

1 x quantity Yorkshire pudding (Yorkie) batter (see Almighty Toad-in-the-hole recipe on page 68)

vegetable oil, for the tin

1 x 400g can thick custard

3 tbsp hazelnut chocolate spread (I like Nutella)

3 tbsp raspberry jam

handful of toffee popcorn, chopped, or 1 tbsp chopped roasted hazelnuts

Make your Yorkie batter a couple of hours before cooking to let it rest.

Preheat the oven to 210°C fan/230°C/gas mark 8.

When it's time to cook, add a little vegetable oil to 9 cups of a Yorkshire pudding tin (add just enough oil to cover the bottom of each). Place in the oven at full whack to heat up for 10 minutes until smoking.

Take the tin out, give the batter a quick stir, then pour some batter into each cup to come about a third of the way up. Return to the oven, then reduce the oven temperature to 200°C fan/220°C/gas mark 7 and cook the Yorkies for around 15-20 minutes. Do not open the oven door. When the Yorkies are golden and risen, open the oven door for 5 seconds, then shut it. Turn off the oven and leave the Yorkies in there for 15 minutes, then take them out and let them cool in the tin for 30 minutes.

Once cooled, place the Yorkies on a large plate, then pipe or spoon the custard into the dip in the middle of the Yorkies. Put the hazelnut chocolate spread in a bowl and microwave on Medium-Low for 30 seconds to loosen it, then drizzle over the Yorkies. Do the same with the jam. Sprinkle the popcorn or chopped nuts all over the Yorkies, then chill in the fridge for about an hour to firm them up before serving.

THE PEAR OF THE COB – PEAR COBBLER

SERVES 6

This is nice after a big Sunday roast, sitting in front of the fire chatting to family and friends on a cold winter's day. Heaven.

1.2kg ripe pears
50g salted butter
100g caster sugar
½ tsp ground cinnamon
¼ tsp ground nutmeg
good pinch of pepper
100ml dry cider
250g plain flour
1 tbsp baking powder
250ml milk
1 egg
1 tsp vanilla extract
2 Snickers bars

Preheat the oven to 180°C fan/200°C/gas mark 6.

Peel, quarter and core the pears. Add the butter and 50g of the sugar to a saucepan, melt over a low-medium heat, then add the pears and give them a stir. Now stir in the cinnamon, nutmeg and pepper and cook for 5 minutes. Using a slotted spoon, transfer the pears into an ovenproof dish (approx. 28 x 23 x 6cm). Now add the cider to the syrup mixture that's in the saucepan. Turn the heat up and reduce the syrup mixture slightly, about 7-8 minutes, then pour all over the pears. Put to one side.

In a bowl, mix together the flour, baking powder and the remaining 50g sugar. In a separate bowl, mix together the milk, egg and vanilla extract. Gradually pour the egg mix into the flour mix, a bit at a time, and keep stirring/whisking until combined to make a batter. Don't over-whisk the batter - some lumps are fine.

Now take the Snickers bars and cut into bite-sized pieces, then arrange in among the pears. Pour over the cobbler batter to cover the pears evenly.

Bake in the oven for around 25 minutes. It's done when the top is nice and golden and a knife inserted into the cobbler topping comes out clean. Serve hot. This is nice with ice cream.

CARROT CAKE

SERVES 10

The oil in this cake makes it so moist and unctuous and the smell in the kitchen when it's baking is bang on. It's one of them cakes to enjoy when you've just been out for a walk on a cold winter's day, knowing when you get back you can put your feet up in front of the fire and have a slice of cake and a cuppa tea.

200g plain flour

2½ tsp baking powder

½ tsp ground cinnamon

½ tsp ground nutmeg

¼ tsp salt

¼ tsp pepper

2 large eggs

150g caster sugar

100ml vegetable oil

1 tsp vanilla extract

240g carrots, peeled and grated (peeled weight)

60g hazelnuts, chopped

Preheat the oven to 190°C fan/210°C/gas mark 6½. Line a 22 x 12 x 6cm loaf tin with greaseproof paper, making sure you have a 5cm overhang on all sides.

In a bowl, mix the flour, baking powder, cinnamon, nutmeg, salt and pepper together. Put to one side.

In a separate bowl, mix the eggs and sugar together until the sugar has just dissolved. Add the vegetable oil and vanilla and mix until just incorporated, but don't over-mix. Now slowly add the egg mix to the flour mix, but instead of whisking, fold it in with a spatula. Add the carrots and nuts and fold in. Spoon the cake mixture into the prepared loaf tin and level the top.

Bake in the oven for 50-60 minutes. The cake is done when it's nice and golden - when you insert a cocktail stick (or fine skewer) into the middle, it should come out clean.

Remove from the oven and let the cake stand in the tin for 1 hour, then take it out, place on a wire rack and let it stand for 30 minutes before serving. Slice it up and enjoy.

 This cake keeps well, wrapped in foil, for up to 5 days (if it lasts that long!).

LIV & TOBY'S RICE KRISPIE BIRTHDAY 'CAKE'

MAKES AROUND 15-20 PIECES

I've been doing this for as long as I can remember and have been making this 'cake' for Liv and Toby for every one of their birthdays! Still doing it now even when Liv and Toby are adults. It's one I will do forever. I love my kids.

60g unsalted butter

350g marshmallows

250g crispy rice cereal (I use value or own-brand Rice Krispies)

400g milk chocolate (I like Cadbury's), roughly chopped or broken into pieces

hundreds-and-thousands sprinkles, to decorate

Line a 28 x 23 x 6cm dish with greaseproof paper, making sure it goes up all the sides. I scrunch up my greaseproof paper before using it to line the tin; this makes the paper more manageable and you can press it into the corners. Set aside.

Melt the butter in a large saucepan over a medium-low heat. Add the marshmallows and keep stirring until they're all melted and the mix is nice and smooth. Add the crispy rice cereal and mix well so it's all coated. Now spoon the mixture into the lined dish. Take a spatula and keep wetting it with water as you press the mixture down until it is all level and smooth. Now refrigerate for 1 hour to firm up.

Place the chocolate in a heatproof bowl and melt in a microwave on Low in 30-second bursts. Keep checking and stirring every 30 seconds until you have nice smooth melted chocolate.

Take the crispy mixture out of the fridge and pour the chocolate all over the top, spreading it out to cover the top completely. Now sprinkle over the sprinkles to decorate and then place the 'cake' back in the fridge for a couple of hours to set.

Once set, remove from the dish with the help of the lining paper, place on a chopping board and cut into pieces (squares or bars) of whatever size you want. I normally get around 15-20 pieces, depending what size you cut.

Store any leftovers in an airtight container - they keep well for up to a week in the fridge.

DRUNKEN PEARS

SERVES 2

I love this dessert. I love how the cream melts into the syrup, and the saltiness the nuts bring to the party is perfect.

200ml dry cider

4 tbsp light soft brown sugar

5cm piece of fresh ginger, peeled and sliced

½ tsp ground nutmeg

½ tsp ground cinnamon

¼ tsp chilli flakes

zest of 1 small lemon

2 large ripe pears

100ml double cream

1 tbsp icing sugar

¼ tsp vanilla extract

1 tbsp salted cashew nuts

salt and pepper

In a saucepan, combine the cider, 200ml of water, the brown sugar, ginger, nutmeg, cinnamon, chilli flakes, lemon zest and a pinch each of salt and pepper. Bring to the boil over a medium heat, then turn down to a simmer.

Peel and cut the pears in half lengthways, then remove the core. Add the pear halves to the cider syrup mixture, then poach gently for around 15-20 minutes until the pears are just tender. Using a slotted spoon, remove the pear halves to a dish and put to one side.

Now turn the heat up to high and boil the syrup until it is reduced by half, about 8-10 minutes.

Meanwhile, add the cream, icing sugar and vanilla to a bowl. Whip together until nice soft peaks form (but don't over-whip). Now put the nuts into a food bag and bash with a rolling pin into chunky bits.

To serve, arrange 2 pear halves on each serving plate or in each bowl. Spoon the syrup all over. Now spoon the whipped cream on top and sprinkle with the nuts - I like the saltiness the nuts bring to the party.

RASPBERRY & CREAM CHEESE PUFF TART

SERVES 8-10

This is a great family dessert or perfect for feeding a small crowd. It's not too sweet - I like to taste the tartness of the raspberries, but just add more sugar to taste in the sauce if you want it sweeter.

1 x 375g pack ready-rolled puff pastry (1 sheet)

5 tbsp caster sugar

500g frozen raspberries

250ml double cream

2 tsp vanilla extract

165g cream cheese

1 tbsp chopped roasted hazelnuts

10g dark chocolate

salt and pepper

Preheat the oven to 180°C fan/200°C/gas mark 6.

Unroll the puff pastry sheet onto a lined baking tray. With a sharp knife, score all the way around the pastry 2.5cm in from the edge so it's like a picture frame. Do not cut all the way through the pastry. Take a cocktail stick or fork and prick the pastry all over inside the border. Bake in the oven for 15-20 minutes. It will be cooked when it has puffed up and is nice and golden. Remove from the oven and put to one side to cool on the tray.

Meanwhile, in a saucepan, combine 50ml of water and 3 tablespoons of the sugar. Cook over a medium heat until the sugar has dissolved, then add the raspberries (you don't need to defrost them first). Now add a pinch each of salt and pepper. Cook it down for about 6-8 minutes until it's slightly reduced but not to a mush, and keep stirring. Set aside to cool completely.

Take your cooled puff pastry and place it on a serving plate/board. With the back of a spatula, push the puff pastry down inside the border around the edge (so you leave a raised border all the way around). This enables you to fill it more.

Now in a bowl, whip the cream until it forms soft peaks, then stir in the vanilla. In a separate bowl, add the cream cheese and the remaining 2 tablespoons of sugar and beat together until the sugar has dissolved. Now gently fold half the cheese mixture into the whipped cream. Repeat with the rest of the cheese mixture but don't over-work it. Just fold it through to combine.

Spread the cream mixture all over the pastry case inside the raised border. Now spread the raspberry sauce mixture over the creamy layer. Sprinkle the nuts on top, then grate the chocolate all over. Refrigerate for 30 minutes to firm up a bit. This is best eaten on the day it's made as it doesn't keep well. Serve in slices.

BANANA SPLIT

SERVES 2

This dessert is nostalgia at its finest. Naughty but nice. The kids will love this!

2 ripe bananas

6 scoops of Neapolitan ice cream (2 scoops of each flavour – vanilla, chocolate and strawberry)

1 chocolate flake

1 shortbread finger

1 Twix finger

squirty cream

chocolate syrup

strawberry syrup

2 tbsp chopped roasted hazelnuts

2 glacé cherries

Peel the bananas and slice each in half lengthways. For each dessert, place 2 banana halves on a plate or in a fancy bowl/plate if you have one. Now take one scoop of each flavour of the ice cream (vanilla, chocolate and strawberry) and place on the banana halves with gaps in between.

Now chop up your flake, shortbread finger and Twix. Squirt cream in between the ice cream and on the ends and drizzle chocolate and strawberry syrup all over. Now scatter some chopped flake, shortbread and Twix all over, followed by the chopped nuts. Place a glacé cherry on the cream in the middle of each dessert. Dig in and enjoy.

THE DODGER - BANOFFEE PIE

SERVES 6

Always goes down well does a banoffee pie. Incorporating the Jammie Dodger into the base works really well and it gets people thinking.

100g plain digestive biscuits

100g chocolate digestive biscuits

100g jam sandwich biscuits, such as Jammie Dodgers

125g unsalted butter

70g soft dark brown sugar

1 x 375g can condensed milk

270ml double cream

1 tbsp icing sugar

1 large ripe banana or 2-3 small ripe bananas, peeled and chopped

1 tbsp chopped roasted hazelnuts

5g dark chocolate

Place all the biscuits into a food processor and blitz until you have a crumb mixture. If you don't have a food processor, put them into a food bag and smash with a rolling pin. Now put the crumb mixture into a bowl. Melt 50g of the butter and pour over the crumbs, then stir together well until combined. Now spread the crumb mixture into a 20cm round (4cm deep) loose-based cake tin, making sure to cover all up the sides as well. Chill in the fridge for 30 minutes to firm up, then take it out and put to one side.

Put the remaining 75g of butter and the brown sugar into a saucepan over a medium heat and cook until the butter has melted and the sugar has dissolved. Now turn the heat up, then stir in the condensed milk until combined. Bring to the boil and boil for a minute or two – it should start to thicken. Once it has thickened, pour it over the crumb base. Now let it cool for 15 minutes, then chill in the fridge for 1½ hours to firm up.

Once firm, take the pie out of the fridge and put to one side. Pour the cream into a bowl, add the icing sugar and whip together until you have fairly firm peaks, but do not over-whip. Now fold your bananas through the cream, then spoon this mixture all over the pie. Sprinkle the hazelnuts on top, then grate the chocolate all over. Return to the fridge for at least an hour to firm up before serving. Serve in slices (see Tip).

When serving, I find it easier to take a can of beans out of the cupboard and put the can onto the worktop. Place the pie tin on top and gently push down to release the base of the tin away from the sides, then transfer the pie (still on the tin base) to a plate to serve.

THE FOND ONE – COKE FLOAT ICE CREAM SODA

MAKES 2

This is not much of a recipe but I've got fond memories of this. When I was younger, I used to go round to a mate's house and his mam would make a similar one for us. So I feel this deserves to have a place in my book for memories alone. Happy memories.

ice cubes

1 litre cola

1 x 33g bag Magic Stars

12 small scoops of Neapolitan ice cream (4 scoops of each flavour - vanilla, chocolate and strawberry)

chopped roasted hazelnuts

chocolate syrup

strawberry syrup

Take 2 pint (600ml) glasses and put a handful of ice cubes into each glass. Fill the glasses three-quarters of the way up with cola.

Add some Magic Stars. Put 3 small scoops of ice cream (one of each flavour) into each glass. Add some more Magic Stars and some nuts, then squirt some chocolate and strawberry syrup over. Add 3 more small scoops of ice cream, and some more Magic Stars, nuts and syrups.

Serve each with a long spoon and a straw. Enjoy.

THE AFTERBURN - CHILLI CHOCOLATE BARK

SERVES 6-8

Pure enjoyment in a bite. Chilli and chocolate go so well together. It's like cheese and onion, ham and mustard - they were meant to be. I called this the afterburn because it doesn't blow ya head off after eating a piece, it gives you just enough of a burn to know it's there - I love it when you get the kick of chilli after eating. So, so nice. This bark is also great for a gift at Crimbo. Pack into fancy bags and label.

300g milk chocolate

1 tsp chilli flakes

150g white chocolate

100g crispy M&Ms

1 tbsp chopped roasted hazelnuts

½ tsp smoked flaky sea salt

hundreds-and-thousands sprinkles, to decorate

Line a 26 x 20cm baking tray with greaseproof paper.

Put some water in a saucepan over a low heat. Place a heatproof bowl on the top, making sure it's not touching the water underneath (this is a bain-marie). Now break up the milk chocolate and place in the bowl. Leave until melted, stirring occasionally. Once melted, add the chilli flakes and stir. Spread the milk chocolate all over the lined baking tray.

Now break the white chocolate into pieces and put into a separate heatproof bowl. Melt in the microwave on Low in 30-second bursts, stirring after each burst, until fully melted. I do it this way as there are no cocoa solids in white chocolate, just cocoa butter, so it melts better in a microwave. Once melted, blob the white chocolate all over the milk chocolate, then with a cocktail stick or skewer, make fancy swirls.

Now add the M&Ms and dot them about over the surface, then sprinkle the nuts, salt and sprinkles all over. Refrigerate for 2 hours or more to firm up. Once it's firm, break the bark up into pieces.

 tip You can use normal sea salt instead of smoked, if you prefer. This bark keeps well - store in an airtight container in the fridge for up to 2 weeks.

GRANNY D'S WEEKENDER EGG CUSTARD TART

SERVES 6-8

Granny D used to make this every weekend when we were growing up. Me and my brothers and sister used to absolutely love it and we still do to this day. Proper old-school. Using lard and margarine gives the pastry old-school value, too. Store in an airtight container in the fridge and eat within 3 days.

225g plain flour, plus extra for dusting

50g lard

50g margarine

125g caster sugar

pinch of salt

3 large eggs

300ml full-fat milk

1 tsp vanilla extract

¼ tsp ground nutmeg

In a bowl, add the flour, lard, margarine, 25g of the sugar and the salt. Rub the ingredients together with your fingers to a crumb consistency. Stir in 3 tablespoons of water, bringing the pastry together. Turn the dough out onto a floured surface and knead for a minute or two to bring it together fully. Don't over-knead. Press into a ball, wrap in clingfilm and chill in the fridge for 30 minutes. Preheat the oven to 180°C fan/200°C/gas mark 6.

Once the pastry is chilled, roll it out on a lightly floured surface to fit a 20cm round (4cm deep) loose-based tart tin, making sure it is a little bigger than the tin. The pastry should be the thickness of a pound coin. Line the tin with the pastry, making sure you have overhang all the way round. Prick the base all over with a fork. Scrunch up greaseproof paper, then open it out, place it in the pastry case and fill up with dried rice or baking beans.

Blind-bake for 10 minutes. Remove from the oven and take out the paper and rice/beans. Return the pastry case to the oven, uncovered, and bake for another 10 minutes until golden. Remove from the oven. With a sharp knife, trim away the overhang so it's flush and then put the pastry case to one side.

In a heatproof bowl, whisk together the remaining 100g of sugar and the eggs. Warm the milk in a saucepan until just about boiling, then pour it over the sugar and eggs in a constant flow, stirring all the time until combined. Stir in the vanilla. Strain the mixture into the pastry case, then sprinkle with the nutmeg.

Bake for 10 minutes, then turn the temperature down to 100°C fan/120°C/gas mark ½ and cook for another 10 minutes. The tart is cooked when the custard is set but still has a nice wobble to it. Remove from the oven and leave to cool to room temperature, then refrigerate for 1 hour to set fully before serving.

CONVERSION CHARTS

LIQUID MEASURES

METRIC	IMPERIAL	METRIC	IMPERIAL
1.25ml	¼ tsp	400ml	14fl oz
2.5ml	½ tsp	450ml	15fl oz (¾ pint)
5ml	1 tsp	475ml	16fl oz
15ml	1 tbsp	500ml	18fl oz
30ml	1fl oz (2 tbsp)	600ml	20fl oz (1 pint)
50ml	2fl oz	700ml	1¼ pints (25fl oz)
75ml	3fl oz	850ml	1½ pints (30fl oz)
100ml	3½fl oz	1 litre	1¾ pints (35fl oz)
125ml	4fl oz	1.2 litres	2 pints (40fl oz)
150ml	5fl oz (¼ pint)	1.3 litres	2¼ pints
175ml	6fl oz	1.4 litres	2½ pints
200ml	7fl oz	1.75 litres	3 pints
250ml	8fl oz	2 litres	3½ pints
275ml	9fl oz	3 litres	5 pints
300ml	10fl oz (½ pint)		
325ml	11fl oz		
350ml	12fl oz		
375ml	13fl oz		

SPOONS

1 tsp	5ml
1 dsp	10ml
1 tbsp (3 tsp)	15ml

DRY WEIGHTS

METRIC	IMPERIAL	METRIC	IMPERIAL	METRIC	IMPERIAL
10g	¼oz	250g	9oz	1.25kg	2¾lb
15g	½oz	275g	9½oz	1.3kg	3lb
20g	¾oz	300g	11oz	1.5kg	3¼lb
25g	1oz	350g	12oz	1.6kg	3½lb
40g	1½oz	375g	13oz	1.8kg	4lb
50g	2oz	400g	14oz	2kg	4½lb
60g	2¼oz	425g	15oz		
70g	2¾oz	450g	16oz (1lb)		
75g	3oz	500g	1lb 2oz		
100g	3½oz	550g	1¼lb		
115g	4oz	600g	1lb 5oz		
125g	4½oz	675g	1½lb		
140g	4¾oz	725g	1lb 10oz		
150g	5oz	800g	1¾lb		
160g	5½oz	850g	1lb 14oz		
175g	6oz	900g	2lb		
200g	7oz	1kg	2¼lb		
225g	8oz (½lb)	1.1kg	2½lb		

OVEN TEMPERATURES

ELECTRICITY °C	ELECTRICITY (FAN) °C	°F	GAS MARK	
140°C	120°C	275°F	1	Cool
150°C	130°C	300°F	2	
160°C	140°C	325°F	3	Moderate
180°C	160°C	350°F	4	
190°C	170°C	375°F	5	Moderately Hot
200°C	180°C	400°F	6	
220°C	200°C	425°F	7	Hot
230°C	210°C	450°F	8	
240°C	220°C	475°F	9	Very Hot

INDEX

INDEX

INDEX

SHOUT-OUTS

Donna, Liv, Toby, Kyle and granddaughter, beautiful Saylor Rose. You are my world, my happiness, my everything xxxxx

To my mum Eunice, brothers and sisters, Dale, Jonny, Mark, Emma and Karen, and partners Karen, Kate, Jane, Dan and Dan. And my beautiful nieces and nephews, Darcey, Jett, Lily, Harry, Jake and Lola x

Special thanks to my mum and Jonny for always being there for me, looking after me and supporting me, it means the world to me x

To Nige and Carol, Roofer Paul, Jamie and Jade, Nick (Goody) and Emma, and Ken who is sadly no longer with us all (gone but never forgotten) x

Big shout out to Lisa and Louise and all the team at HarperCollins HQ for giving me this amazing opportunity and believing in me. I will be forever grateful x

Thanks to the team at Bev James - Bev, Tom, Aoife, Emily and Liz - for looking after me so well and supporting me. True professionals, but great friends as well. Sorry for all the late-night messages, Tom (about me worrying about the book!) x

Thanks to Martin for your amazing photography. I certainly made the right choice, that's for sure. Thanks to Lydia, Kim, Grace, Laura and Stevie for the styling and cooking - absolutely on point. I had such a blast shooting the book. Thank you all so much xx. PS: Thanks for digging the Sergio Tacchini, Martin.

Finally, I would like to thank the main man, Jamie Oliver, and all his team at Jamie's HQ for supporting me along the way. Top, top people.

Big love to you all xx

When using kitchen appliances please always follow
the manufacturer's instructions.

HQ
An imprint of HarperCollins*Publishers* Ltd
1 London Bridge Street
London SE1 9GF

www.harpercollins.co.uk

HarperCollins*Publishers*
Macken House
39/40 Mayor Street Upper
Dublin 1
D01 C9W8
Ireland

10 9 8 7 6 5 4 3 2 1

First published in Great Britain by
HQ, an imprint of HarperCollins*Publishers* Ltd 2024

Text copyright © Ian Bursnall 2024
Photography copyright © Martin Poole 2024

Ian Bursnall asserts the moral right to be
identified as the author of this work.
A catalogue record for this book is
available from the British Library.

ISBN: 978-0-00-858018-6

This book is produced from independently certified
FSC™ paper to ensure responsible forest management.

For more information visit:
www.harpercollins.co.uk/green

Photographer: Martin Poole
Food Stylist: Kim Morphew
Prop Stylist: Lydia McPherson
Design Director: Laura Russell
Layout Designer: Nicky Collings
Publishing Director: Louise McKeever
Editor: Rachael Kilduff
Copy-editor: Anne Sheasby
Senior Production Controller: Halema Begum
Printed and bound in India